TWENTIETH CENTURY FAITH

Hope and Survival

RELIGIOUS PERSPECTIVES

Planned and Edited by

RUTH NANDA ANSHEN

RELIGIOUS PERSPECTIVES • *Volume Twenty-five*

TWENTIETH CENTURY FAITH

WITHDRAWN

Hope and Survival

Margaret Mead

The American Museum of Natural History

HARPER & ROW, PUBLISHERS
New York, Evanston, San Francisco, London

FIRST EDITION

STANDARD BOOK NUMBER: 06-065549-6

LIBRARY OF CONGRESS CATALOG CARD NUMBER: 72-78081

Designed by Yvette A. Vogel

RELIGIOUS PERSPECTIVES

VOLUMES ALREADY PUBLISHED

CONTENTS

Religious Perspectives
Its Meaning and Purpose

Religious Perspectives represents a quest for the rediscovery of man. It constitutes an effort to define man's search for the essence of being in order that he may have a knowledge of goals. It is an endeavor to show that there is no possibility of achieving an understanding of man's total nature on the basis of phenomena known by the analytical method alone. It hopes to point to the false antinomy between revelation and reason, faith and knowledge, grace and nature, courage and anxiety. Mathematics, physics, philosophy, biology, and religion, in spite of their almost complete independence, have begun to sense their interrelatedness and to become aware of that mode of cognition which teaches that "the light is not without but within me, and I myself am the light."

My Introduction to this Series is not of course to be construed as a prefatory essay for each individual book. These few pages simply attempt to set forth the general aim and purpose of the Series as a whole. They try to point to the humanistic and transcendent significance of the creative process in the respective disciplines as represented by those schol-

xii | RELIGIOUS PERSPECTIVES

ars who have been invited to participate in this endeavor.

Modern man is threatened by a world created by himself. He is faced with the conversion of mind to naturalism, a dogmatic secularism and an opposition to a belief in the transcendent. He begins to see, however, that the universe is given not as one existing and one perceived but as the unity of subject and object; that the barrier between them cannot be said to have been dissolved as the result of recent experience in the physical sciences, since this barrier has never existed. Confronted with the question of meaning, he is summoned to rediscover and scrutinize the immutable and the permanent which constitute the dynamic, unifying aspect of life as well as the principle of differentiation; to reconcile identity and diversity, immutability and unrest. He begins to recognize that just as every person descends by his particular path, so he is able to ascend, and this ascent aims at a return to the source of creation, an inward home from which he has become estranged.

It is the hope of RELIGIOUS PERSPECTIVES that the rediscovery of man will point the way to the rediscovery of God. To this end a rediscovery of first principles should constitute part of the quest. These principles, not to be superseded by new discoveries, are not those of historical worlds that come to be and perish. They are to be sought in the heart and spirit of man, and no interpretation of a merely historical or scientific universe can guide the search. RELIGIOUS PERSPECTIVES attempts not only to ask dispassionately what the nature of God is, but also to restore to human life at least the hypothesis of God and the symbols that relate to him. It endeavors to show that man is faced with the metaphysical question of the truth of religion while he encounters the empirical question of its effects on the life of humanity and its meaning for society. Religion is here distinguished from theology and its doctrinal forms and is intended to denote the feelings, aspirations, and acts of men, as they relate to total reality. For we are all in search of reality, of a reality which is there whether we know it or not; and the search is of our own making but reality is not.

RELIGIOUS PERSPECTIVES is nourished by the spiritual and intellectual energy of world thought, by those religious and ethical leaders who are not merely spectators but scholars deeply involved in the critical problems common to all religions. These thinkers recognize that human morality and human ideals thrive only when set in a context of a transcendent attitude toward religion and that by pointing to the ground of identity and the common nature of being in the religious experience of man, the essential nature of religion may be defined. Thus, they are committed to reevaluate the meaning of everlastingness, an experience which has been lost and which is the content of that *visio Dei* constituting the structure of all religions. It is the many absorbed everlastingly into the ultimate unity, a unity subsuming what Whitehead calls the fluency of God and the everlastingness of passing experience.

The false dichotomies, created by man, especially Western man, do not exist in nature. Antinomies are unknown in the realm of nature. The new topology of the earth implies the link between an act and a whole series of consequences; and a consciousness of the individual that every time a decision is made it has distant consequences which become more precisely determined.

Furthermore, man has a desire for "elsewhere," a third dimension which cannot be found on earth and yet which must be experienced on earth: prediction: detailed statement referring to something that is to happen in the future; projection: combining a number of trends; prevision: that which is scientifically probable and likely to happen; prospective: the relation between present activity and the image of the future; plan: the sum of total decisions for coordinated activities with a goal in mind.

The authors in RELIGIOUS PERSPECTIVES attempt to show

that to *be* is more important than to have since *being* leads to transcendence and joy, while having only leads to apathy and despair.

Man has now reached the point of controlling those forces both outside himself and within himself which throughout history hemmed in decision-making. And what is decisive is that this new trend is irreversible. We have eaten of this new tree of knowledge and what fifty years ago seemed *fate* has now become the subject of our deliberate choices. Therefore, for man, both in the East and in the West, the two basic questions are: What proper use can we make of our knowledge both for the spirit and for the body and what are the criteria for our choices? Only the answers to these questions, which conform to the new reality, can assure the continuity of human life and preserve the human person who is related not only to the present but also to the past and therefore to the future in a meaningful existence. The choice is ours—a choice between perfection of performance or, and more important, the acceptance of spiritual and moral conduct.

These volumes seek to show that the unity of which we speak consists in a certitude emanating from the nature of man who seeks God and the nature of God who seeks man. Such certitude bathes in an intuitive act of cognition, participating in the divine essence and is related to the natural spirituality of intelligence. This is not by any means to say that there is an equivalence of all faiths in the traditional religions of human history. It is, however, to emphasize the distinction between the spiritual and the temporal which all religions acknowledge. For duration of thought is composed of instants superior to time, and is an intuition of the permanence of existence and its meta-historical reality. In fact, the symbol* itself found on cover and jacket of each volume of RELIGIOUS PERSPECTIVES is the

*From the original design by Leo Katz.

visible sign or representation of the essence, immediacy, and timelessness of religious experience; the one immutable center, which may be analogically related to being in pure act, moving with centrifugal and ecumenical necessity outward into the manifold modes, yet simultaneously, with dynamic centripetal power and with full intentional energy, returning to the source. Through the very diversity of its authors, the Series shows that the basic and poignant concern of every faith is to point to, and overcome the crisis in our apocalyptic epoch—the crisis of man's separation from man and of man's separation from God —the failure of love. The authors endeavor, moreover, to illustrate the truth that the human heart is able, and even yearns, to go to the very lengths of God; that the darkness and cold, the frozen spiritual misery of recent times are breaking, cracking, and beginning to move, yielding to efforts to overcome spiritual muteness and moral paralysis. In this way, it is hoped, the immediacy of pain and sorrow, the primacy of tragedy and suffering in human life, may be transmuted into a spiritual and moral triumph. For the uniqueness of man lies in his capacity for self-transcendence.

RELIGIOUS PERSPECTIVES is therefore an effort to explore the *meaning* of God, an exploration which constitutes an aspect of man's intrinsic nature, part of his ontological substance. This Series grows out of an abiding concern that in spite of the release of man's creative energy which science has in part accomplished, this very science has overturned the essential order of nature. Shrewd as man's calculations have become concerning his means, his choice of ends which was formerly correlated with belief in God, with absolute criteria of conduct, has become witless. God is not to be treated as an exception to metaphysical principles, invoked to prevent their collapse. He is rather their chief exemplification, the sources of all potentiality. The personal reality of freedom and providence, of will and conscience, may demonstrate that "he who knows" commands a depth of consciousness inaccessible to the profane man, and is capable of that transfiguration which prevents the twisting of all good to ignominy. This religious content of experience is not within the province of science to bestow; it corrects the error of treating the scientific account as if it were itself metaphysical or religious; it challenges the tendency to make a religion of science—or a science of religion—a dogmatic act which destroys the moral dynamic of man. Indeed, many men of science are confronted with unexpected implications of their own thought and are beginning to accept, for instance, the trans-spatial and trans-temporal dimension in the nature of reality.

RELIGIOUS PERSPECTIVES attempts to show the fallacy of the apparent irrelevance of God in history. This Series submits that no convincing image of man can arise, in spite of the many ways in which human thought has tried to reach it, without a philosophy of human nature and human freedom which does not exclude God. This image of *Homo cum Deo* implies the highest conceivable freedom, the freedom to step into the very fabric of the universe, a new formula for man's collaboration with the creative process and the only one which is able to protect man from the terror of existence. This image implies further that the mind and conscience are capable of making genuine discriminations and thereby may reconcile the serious tensions between the secular and religious, the profane and sacred. The idea of the sacred lies in what it *is*, timeless existence. By emphasizing timeless existence against reason as a reality, we are liberated in our communion with the eternal, from the otherwise unbreakable rule of "before and after." Then we are able to admit that all forms, all symbols in religions, by their negation of error and their affirmation of the actuality of truth, make it possible to experience that *knowing* which is above knowledge, and that dynamic passage of the universe to unending unity.

God is here interpreted not as a heteronomous being issuing commandments but as the *Tatt-Twam-Asi:* "Do unto others as you would have others do unto you. For I am the Lord." This does not mean a commandment from on high but rather a self-realization through "the other"; since the isolated individual is unthinkable and meaningless. Man becomes man by recognizing his true nature as a creature capable of will and decision. For then the divine and the sacred become manifest. And though he believes in choices, he is no Utopian expecting the "coming of the kingdom." Man, individually and collectively, is losing the chains which have bound him to the inexorable demands of nature. The constraints are diminishing and an infinity of choices becomes available to him. Thus man himself, from the sources of his ontological being, at last must decide what is the *bonum et malum.* And though the anonymous forces which in the past have set the constraints do indeed threaten him with total anarchy and with perhaps a worse tyranny than he experienced in past history, he nevertheless begins to see that preceding the moral issue is the cognitive problem: the perception of those conditions for life which permit mankind to fulfill itself and to accept the truth that beyond scientific, discursive knowledge is nondiscursive, intuitive awareness. And, I suggest, this is not to secularize God but rather to gather him into the heart of the nature of matter and indeed of life itself.

The volumes in this Series seek to challenge the crisis which separates, to make reasonable a religion that binds, and to present the numinous reality within the experience of man. Insofar as the Series succeeds in this quest, it will direct mankind toward a reality that is eternal and away from a preoccupation with that which is illusory and ephemeral.

We are in the presence of a serious crisis of knowledge. This crisis could be defined as the end of social determinism or the end of social fatalism. In other words, our era, for the last two generations, represents a fundamental break with all past history. For we now possess a rapidly growing ability to control the forces which throughout history hemmed in individual decision-making and, even more important, which made the collective social processes appear as inexorable events ruled by pseu-do-natural laws.

Up to the middle of the nineteenth century, for example, the population trend was ruled by nothing but biological laws, and the balance of population was regulated by "natural" events such as Malthus' three horsemen: war, hunger, pestilence. Now a change has been brought about not only by individual control of birth rates and death rates, but also by collective application of public health policies and the findings of epidemiology. Other examples of equal significance could be mentioned.

Here, however, I wish to refer to a trend which takes us back to the Renaissance. During the last two generations we have made a quantum jump, or, in Hegelian terms, the quantitative changes have altered the quality of our life world. And what is decisive is that this trend of which I speak is *irreversible*. We have eaten of this new tree of knowledge, and what fifty years ago appeared to be *fate* has now become the subject of our deliberate choices.

So, if choices are to be made, the first question is: on what foundations of knowledge? And the second question obviously is: what are the criteria for our choices? Our dilemma is one of criteria for our judgments. And it is the hope of RELIGIOUS PERSPECTIVES to try to point to at least some of them.

For man is now confronted with his burden and his greatness: "He calleth to me, Watchman, what of the night? Watchman, what of the night?"* Perhaps the anguish in the human soul may be assuaged by the answer, by the *assimilation* of the person in God: "The morning cometh, and also the night: if ye will inquire, inquire ye: return, come."**

RUTH NANDA ANSHEN

*Isaiah 21:11.
**Isaiah 21:12.

TWENTIETH CENTURY FAITH

Hope and Survival

1 Cherishing the Life of the World *(1960)*

Through the ages religion has defined our aspirations, but only as our scientific knowledge and understanding of man has increased, have we been able to put them into effect. The admonition to care for the sick and feed the hungry could be fulfilled by a few acts of kindness and occasional alms that did only a little to stem the tide of illness and death, and rescue the starving peoples of the world—until our modern knowledge of disease, and our modern knowledge of food and agriculture, made these a greater reality. The religious motive, the vision of a better world in which man could care for his neighbor more, has always come first. Our vision is not clearer or greater because it can now be implemented by science. But it is very much *surer.* The will to care for the leper is no greater than when Father Damian set sail, but today leprosy can be arrested and finally eradicated from a whole population.

Spiritual health is the name we have given to our new goals for mankind which stress not so much the welfare of the body, as the welfare of the mind and spirit. The new understandings, the new methods of diagnosis and treatment of the ills of the mind, stem from many disciplines, psychiatry, the behavioral sciences, the study of cultures and society, the minute study of nerve and brain. It is the banner beneath which those of us who are scientists and those of us who work in specifically religious fields can forget our narrower professional allegiances, the limitations of our national identity, the specific loyalties of time and place.

In this way members of different faiths work together for a common goal, and differences become strengths in furthering that goal, rather than barriers between us. All over the world, this is what we want to do with differences, of nationality, of religious belief, of scientific discipline: use the strengths which are given by working within a special set of loyalties, and learn to keep these differences from dividing us. The great religions of the world have become great because those who embraced them were willing to cross every barrier in carrying their vision to other men, different in race, in language, in culture. Religious groups are the only completely inclusive voluntary groups in the world, in which people of every age, both sexes, every walk of life, every degree of education, are included together as members of one body. It is these aspects of religion—the recognition that all men are brothers, the willingness to seek out men of other kinds and draw them in, the inclusion of a people within a voluntary association—that will provide great strength to the spiritual, moral, and mental health of mankind.

All over the world, in fifty-two countries, the peoples of countries as diverse as England and Japan, France and Thailand, Denmark and the Philippines, in the countries of the Caribbean, in South America, in Australia and New Zealand, groups of people who have come to share a common goal for mankind are working under the banner of the spiritual health of the human race.

Within the new possibilities of analysis and procedure provided by science, humanity can begin to face the overwhelming responsibilities of this period of human history, when the great religious truth of the unity of all mankind must be actualized, or the people perish—all of them everywhere in the world. For the first time in our known human history, the whole of mankind is caught in one fate; each man is indeed his brother's keeper, and the need to love our enemies must be given new concrete scientific and religious meaning. Only if we are able to love—in the sense of cherish and protect, although not agree with—those who are our enemies, while they are our enemies, can we hope to protect the lives of men and the life of the world. Spiritual health is a goal for all mankind, not for separate groups or classes, not for the members of particular nations or countries or blocs; for the world, as for the individual, the will to cherish that springs from religious faith, needs the implementation of science and creative social invention. Faith and architectural principles erected our great temples and cathedrals; faith and the human sciences are needed to erect a social order in which the children of our enemies will be protected as surely as our own children, so that all will be safe.

▉▉ Christians in a Technological Era*
(1964)

This book is directed toward those who take religion seriously
—those who cannot conceive of a life bearing a religious label
which is not infused with that religion. At the present time such
people are at a disadvantage in the United States. It is reluc-
tantly recognized that there are those whose lives center on
religion: the clergy (who should not overemphasize the religious aspect of their career), monks and nuns (who seem increasingly out of place in the contemporary American world),
some Roman Catholics (especially those belonging to certain
self-conscious ethnic groups), various separatist sects (whose
members confine their lives within the framework of beliefs
that hold them together and separate them from the world),
and the occasional individual who, as the French would say, is

*This chapter includes comments on a series of papers published under the
title of *Christians in a Technological Era*, ed. Hugh C. White, Jr.: Margaret
Mead, "Introduction"; Michael Polanyi, "The Scientific Revolution"; Jean La-
driere, "Faith and the Technician Mentality"; Bernard Morel, "Science and
Technology in God's Design"; François Russo, "Modern Science and the Christian Faith"; Jean de la Croix Kaelin, "Faith and Technology"; Scott I. Paradise,
"Christian Mission and the Technician Mentality in America."

un person croyant et pieux. But most Americans—even though they acknowledge some slight connection with religion, accept the label of some denomination, and obey a certain set of ritualistic requirements—do not admit the existence of a significant connection between the lives they lead, the careers they pursue, the thoughts they think, and their relationship to God or their spiritual existence.

In this atmosphere the old battles between science and religion—once exemplified in the sturdy atheism of the country editor—are dying away. It is difficult even to obtain a statement of the issues. Most young Americans tend to find absurd any attempt to juxtapose the historic Christian doctrine and our cybernetic age. And for those few who have embraced a religious vocation with enthusiasm, the idea of facing the modern scientific revolution is almost unthinkable; in making their vocational choice they are likely to ignore anything that has been said or thought in the last two hundred years.

For such individuals it is perfectly acceptable to disapprove of television, worry mildly about the unemployment of youth, frown over the increase in juvenile delinquency, lament the decay of morals, criticize "Madison Avenue" (while increasingly adopting Madison Avenue tactics), and denounce subliminal advertising or a book like *Tropic of Cancer.* But it is a different matter altogether to consider seriously the position of the Christian to whom Christianity is a way of life in a world in which men have the power to destroy all human life—to destroy, in fact, all life—and the power to give abundant life to all human beings, powers which once were believed to belong only to God.

It is one of the merits of the ecumenical movement that it endows with new life certain older ways of living and thinking which had become stale and complacent. Furthermore, it is a means of breaking down the barriers of isolation, specialization, and compensatory hostility. In the past the different emphases developed within each particular area of isolation deepened some perceptions while neglecting others. These several insights are now made available to the whole Christian community, and the spirit is uplifted as more of mankind is encompassed in a widened embrace.

So this ecumenical debate—the fundamental premises of which are essentially unfamiliar to most Americans, who are busy with good works and are sustained by unexamined faith—should cut through to the very core of our indifference. The five European discussants* are primarily concerned with intellectual issues but their arguments, considered seriously, should also have meaning for the Christian position on such matters as racial integration, the measures necessary to create a warless world, the responsibility of one generation to the next in ensuring that no irreversible damage is done to soil or air or water, to fish or bird or forest, and the willingness of man to accept a burden perhaps even greater than that laid on humanity when our primal parents first ate of the fruit of the tree of knowledge of good and evil—the burden of responsibility for the survival of life on earth.

At the heart of the discussion is the question of the place of the world in the life and the solicitude of the Christian and the Scriptural grounds for cherishing or rejecting it. In Christian history the world, the flesh, and the Devil have been variously defined, and one of the problems of our era is a reclarification of their interrelationship. Jesus said: "My kingdom is not of this world." Should Christians, therefore, ignore the world? Should they accept the position taken by some clergymen, whom I have heard say, in effect: "Well, you scientists made the bomb. It's up to you to deal with it"? Or the even more fundamentalist position: "This world is filled with sin and iniquity, and the sooner it is destroyed the better"? Should Christians take the

*M. Polanyi, J. Ladrière, B. Morel, I. Russo, J. de la Kaelin.

position that it is the function of this world to "colonize heaven" —and does this mean that the world should be decently run? Are the principalities and the powers not only secular but also essentially profane and the object of Christian avoidance? Or have Christians a responsibility when the law courts mete out a different kind of justice to the rich and to the poor?

And the flesh? For two thousand years Christians, as individuals, have taken to heart the injunction, "Feed the hungry," and have given to the needy in various forms of charity. But because scientific knowledge and the supporting technology were lacking, millions died in famines and epidemics. Even today most Christians find more vivid and appealing the image of the soup kitchen for the victims of poverty or earthquakes or floods or war than they do the plans made by the World Health Organization for the prevention of epidemics or by the Food and Agriculture Organization for an adequate world food supply. Christian compassion on the part of the fortunate and Christian resignation on the part of victims of tribulation still prevail as the true expressions of Christian giving. And many see no inconsistency between their belief in giving and their abhorrence of "socialized medicine," "foreign aid," government-sponsored programs of flood control, or international campaigns to eradicate malaria. This was the issue, more than any other, that led the converted natives of the Admiralty Islands to break away from their missionaries.

And it is on these questions—the stewardship of the earth, the cultivation of the earth as a garden, and the command to feed and heal all men—that the issue is joined. In earlier times the Christian, intent on his own soul and the life of the world to come, might devote himself to giving alms, rescuing orphans, and comforting the dying. These relationships provided a satisfactory dynamic tension within which donor and recipient benefited spiritually. But in the present era the conception of giving must be revised. Is it Christian to insist that it is nobler to minister to the individual sufferer than to use technology to wipe out the disease from which that individual is suffering?

The reverberations of this necessary change in relationship between donor and recipient go far beyond the mere reorganization of local charity or the acceptance of measures of social security essential in our technological era. They ring through the new declaration of the Third Lambeth Conference:*

> Our unity in Christ, expressed in our full communion, is the most profound bond among us, in all our political and racial and cultural diversity.
>
> The time has fully come when this unity and interdependence must find a completely new level of expression and corporate obedience.
>
> Our need is not, therefore, simply to be expressed in greater generosity by those who have money and men to spare. Our need is rather to understand how God has led us, through the sometimes painful history of our time, to see the gifts of freedom and communion in their great terms, and to live up to them. If we are not responsible stewards of what Christ has given us, we will lose even what we have.

The technological capabilities of the modern world have bound together all men, one species in one community, and this new interdependence is creating a climate of opinion in which the older dependence of the have-nots on the benevolence of the haves is being replaced by a new idea of partnership in the use of technology. In international organizations the older societies, which at present have the greatest technical resources, and the newer societies, which need these resources, can work together as partners of equal dignity, members one of another.

Just as in the latter days of Rome the new Christian ethic produced a new technical application when, for the first time, hospitals were established to care for the poor, so today the new technology demands a new ethical application. Yet perhaps at

*1963.

no other time has the gap been so great between the explicit tenets of Christianity and the attempt to utilize in the service of Christian principles the possibilities offered by existing technology. Christian institutions continue to follow an inappropriate, inadequate, and no longer relevant style of individual Christian charity; in doing so, they surrender to the secular world—even the Communist world—the wider goals of feeding the hungry, caring for the sick, and protecting the poor in ways that can lead to the abolition of hunger, chronic illness, and poverty.

The question of whether technology as a whole is to be placed on the side of good or evil is the third of the set of perennial problems with which these discussants are concerned. For Americans, the European emphasis may seem strange, since even those Americans who feel that science may be evil seldom doubt that technology is good. Obdurant and recalcitrant as some Americans are in their attitudes toward Darwinian theory or contemporary astronomical theories of the origins of the universe, they enthusiastically accept almost every technological achievement—the automobile, the airplane, radio, television, refrigeration and air conditioning, plastics and other synthetic materials—and they pause only briefly over the man-made satellite because they do not yet see its usefulness or because the Russians put one into orbit first. The European's deep distrust of the machine, which seems to him to be destroying the "human scale" and man's classic humanity, is very slightly developed in the United States and is seldom encountered here except in the cloistered halls devoted to the humanities. Consequently, this part of the argument will perhaps be mystifying to Americans. They may well ponder and need to investigate further Kaelin's statement that "the Christian must face the real risks which technology causes him to run," for Kaelin is referring to spiritual risks, not (as one might easily assume) the risk of the obliteration of the human race.

However, in spite of the generally acceptant American attitude toward machines—which English Luddites once tried to destroy as the destroyers of their handicraft livelihood—American Christians are in some danger of turning against the new cybernetic machines. Lacking any depth of thinking about the modern world, they may well regard the whole idea of computers and automation as essentially evil and demonic ways of dehumanizing man. Morel's lucid discussion of the scientific basis of automation and of the way in which information theory can be integrated into theology touches the very heart of this issue. He views cybernetics as a new way of describing the organization of the universe, as part of the grand design, and as descriptive of a process going on perhaps even in inanimate matter. Viewed in this way, the cybernetic revolution is not a set of mathematical principles which, in effect, reduce human beings to ciphers in the service of large, power-thirsty aggregations of nuts and bolts. Instead, it is a great leap forward in man's humanity, comparable to other revolutionary advances—man's recognition that tools can be fashioned, that animals can be bred and that seeds can be planted, that the seasons recur, that spoken language can be reduced to written form, that fire need not be feared as an enemy but, domesticated, can be welcomed as a source of safety and comfort.

Christianity happily accepted all these earlier triumphs of man's increasing knowledge of nature—the seed, the plow and the reaper's scythe, the husbandman with his flock, the hearth, the script which made possible the Scriptures. But, it should be noted, these insights, through which man vastly improved the efficiency of his stewardship and increased the extent of his dominion over the earth, came before the Old Testament was written and were firmly incorporated into civilization long before the coming of Christ. And Christianity, which blesses the time-honored forms through which man exercises his intelligence and systematizes his knowledge of nature, shows only a limited capacity to accept new insights and to bless new forms.

Today, as in the past, resistance to new forms of knowledge has its source both in accepted practice and in a general psychological resistance to change in modes of thinking. Automation threatens established interests, such as those of trade unionists —and this at a time when, belatedly, some Christians are learning to appreciate the need for trade unionism. But the greatest immediate challenge is to our mode of thinking about scarcity and plenty: from a central concern with the problem of how to provide a paying job for everyone so that production can be kept up, we must shift to a concern with the problem of how to provide a basis of intelligent consumption for everyone so that our incredible productive capacity can be used. This challenge will have to be met first in the United States, and there is little in traditional American Protestant thought which prepares us to meet it.

The discussions of science deal with problems which are equally urgent and perhaps of even greater interest. The primary emphasis here is on science as an approach to knowledge which has much in common with other approaches to an understanding of the universe. The twentieth century conception of science as a continuing search is a welcome contrast to the earlier static and absolutist conception with its ineluctable conclusion that if science is right, then religion must be wrong. (That this viewpoint still has its adherents is evident in many contemporary discussions of the teaching of evolution.) Absolute revelation, however parochial the interpretation of the vision and archaic the language, confronted absolute truth and this arrogant, exclusive absolutism—shared by scientists and religious thinkers alike—resulted in a stalemate which still paralyzes the thinking of some living scientists and theologians. Phrased in this way, no synthesis—indeed no search for synthesis—was possible.

Beginning with a different phrasing, Polanyi, in his illuminating discussion of the I-Thou dimension and the I-Me dimension as well the I-It dimension developed by the physical sciences, in his lucid statement of the commonality of approach in religion and science, and in his conception of comprehension, moves toward synthesis and transcends older, stiff attempts to work out such a synthesis.

So also Russo's description of scientific method should reassure the humanist even as it delights the mind of the scientist. Particularly important is his recognition of a relatively new aspect of our contemporary pursuit of truth:

> Science as we know it today appears to be increasingly based on a *love of research*. By this we mean that the ideal of the scientist today is not so much the attainment and contemplation of truth as progress towards it, the strain of the whole being to achieve it. . . . At this point science no longer appears as a minor or optional form of occupation on a par with a number of others. It appears as a *vital* activity which man cannot do without, any more than he can do without bread. It constitutes a task in which man possesses himself, frees himself, and knows himself, for the reason that we have just given, that it is his deepest vocation.

But science does not only give us new ways of comprehending the universe and new sources of self-knowledge. Science also, in its application, gives us new ways of meeting our Christian obligations. The sciences of chemistry, biology, and nutrition have given us new ways of obeying the injunction, "Feed my lambs." The development of medicine, epidemiology, virology, and bacteriology has given us new ways to "heal the sick." New concepts of social organization and knowledge of how society functions open to us new ways in which man can "seek first the kingdom of God and his righteousness." And our study of the minds of children is revealing the existence of a human need which is as deep as hunger and thirst, as compelling as the need for rest and the need for love—that is, a need to relate to the universe, a "cosmic sense," through which religion has grown and continually becomes meaningful to man.

There are, however, two points at which, it seems to me, we, with all our luminous modernity and sensitivity, have stopped short of facing major issues. First, there is the problem of justifying involvement in the technological improvement of man's lot through the biblical command giving man "dominion . . . over every living thing that moveth upon the earth" (Gen. 1:28). The idea of *dominion* (as also the term *kingdom*) is obsolete in the modern world. For any definition of science as a means of giving man *dominion*—power over—tends to increase the difficulty of realizing responsibility and of curbing exploitation. But the definition of science as an activity leading toward an understanding of the universe allows for responsibility in the use of that knowledge and for the necessity of curbing the exploitive and destructive possibilities of applied science and technology.

Second, such discussions, illuminated as they are by Christian hope, fail to give adequate recognition to the fundamental change introduced in the world by the development of nuclear, chemical, and biological weapons. Contemporary man not only has knowledge of good and evil; he has as well absolute power to destroy. This man-made power of destruction lays on man a burden he has never before experienced—a burden, like that of the knowledge of good and evil, from which he cannot escape in the foreseeable future. Given this power, the acquisition of an understanding of the natural laws which will enable men to construct, protect, and maintain a warless world is a precondition to all other benefits we may reap from our new knowledge of nature and man himself.

III Christian Faith and Technical Assistance
(1955)

The revolution that has taken place in the last decades in our capacity to speed up technological change has confronted the Christian churches with an ethical dilemma of no small proportions. Throughout the last two thousand years Christianity and Judaism have provided the religious ethic which gave meaning and purpose to the attempts to ease the misery and lighten the darkness of the slave, the serf, the peasant, the heathen, and the aboriginal inhabitants of the newly discovered continents and islands beyond the sea. In the Judaic ethic to heal, to teach, and to feed the poor, were good deeds, benefiting the giver, in fact benefiting the giver to such a degree that the recipient was hardly expected to reciprocate with more than formal deference. Similarly, in traditional Christianity the care of the sick, teaching the ignorant, and feeding the hungry were all works through which individuals, acting in Christian compassion and charity, walked more closely in the ways of the Lord. This position was congruent with the state of technology during the first nineteen hundred years of the Christian Era. Christian compassion for suffering loomed far larger than Christian ability to cure disease; Christian charity might succor and help the needy, but the Great Famines and the Black Death raged across Europe; Christian piety and devotion might reproduce manuscripts by hand, but universal literacy waited upon printing, mass production of books, and the audio-visual methods of the twentieth century. From the kitchens of monasteries and colleges there might be distributions to the poor at Christmas of lumps of meats "the size of a child's head," and within convents the children left after plague and famine swept the land might be lovingly reared. Against plague, famine, and ignorance, these were slender bulwarks indeed. Religion counseled resignation to the will of God, and tempered the bitterness and rebellion of those whose children died one by one in infancy, or remained the sole survivors of some plague. As compassion was the appropriate active Christian virtue for those who ministered to the unfortunate, so resignation was the equally appropriate virtue in those who must bow their heads before a series of misfortunes which we would today account as preventable.

Meanwhile, both compassionate service and gentle resignation were reinforced by an other-worldliness which despised material things, even while distributing bread to the starving, or bathing the terrible sores on the feet of those who had no shoes in winter. This other-worldliness could survive even while using as good symbols those tools by which men gained their bread and journeyed over the seas to obtain new foods— the plow, the sickle, the ship—these were symbols which could be combined with the deepest religious devotion. Then came the machine, the substitution of fuel for men and women walking treadmills, the substitution of mechanical processes for the weariness of human hands. At first the machine seemed to be enslaving the human spirit rather than releasing it. As men and women entered the mines and factories, it seemed clear that the machine was Moloch devouring the souls and bodies of newly urbanized, lost, exploited human beings. The plow, the

sickle, and the sail remained symbols of simple Christian goodness, of the yielding earth, of the good grain reaped in the fields,
and of the traveler for whom one prayed, but the machine
which was to increase the yield of the land and make the jour-
neying traveler safe became identified with Mammon. The machine and all its works were evil—set against the vision of a New
Jerusalem that might instead be built in England's green and
pleasant lands. As the products of the machine grew, and men
came to live in cities which became more identified with god-
lessness, materialism, industrialism, and urbanism became a
trilogy of the works of the Devil—an emphasis which was not
lessened by the emphasis of Bolshevik propaganda upon god-
lessness coupled with the new deification of the machine.

So today we find ourselves in a parlous state. Since World War
II the new technology, combined with the upsurge of aspiration
and hope among all the peoples of the world, means that we
confront a possibility of preventing hunger and premature
death, and of opening up the opportunities of literacy and experience, beyond the wildest dreams of only a few decades ago.
We confront this prospect, not with the full vigor of religious
dedication, but with divided hearts and minds, with a doubt
whether anything born of the machine can be good, with a fear
that it is materialistic to plan, to import tractors, or to set up
assembly lines, to wear mass-produced goods, buy paper books,
or even—for some recently Christianized primitive peoples—
to want shoes. A religious ethic attuned to compassion and
resignation in a world of suffering and poverty is confused and
stumbling in the face of a possible world where no one need go
hungry, or die for want of a known remedy, or go ignorant and
illiterate through life.

Communism and its adherents experience no such confusions. However much their methods may compromise their
ends so that they are unattainable, they are clear in the congruence between health, education, and welfare, on the one hand,

and the Communist ethic on the other, and young Soviet delegates to international congresses are moved to genuine tears by stories of land reclamation in some valley of starving peasants. The full vigor of their belief that food and health education are the most worthwhile ideals to pursue, for themselves and for other people, can go out to meet the awakened hopes of the hungry, ignorant, disease-ridden peoples of the jungles and deserts of the undeveloped countries of the earth. Meanwhile, the minds of Christian missionaries abroad and Christian people at home are divided; in their insistence that men do not live by bread alone, they are unwilling to let their hearts be kindled by the possibility that all men may have bread. All too often enthusiasts who are dedicating themselves to the cause of technical assistance, fighting for more appropriations, seeking to develop ways and means of harnessing the skills of part of the modern world to the service of the rest of the world, must work with only their own secular zeal to sustain them, without benefit or backing from the churches. "The mission told us the Truth, but they did not show us the way," say the awakening peoples of the Pacific Islands, rebelling against teaching which told them "the Truth about the beginning of the world," but did not "tell us how to keep our babies from dying or our people from dying as young men."

The failure of the Christian churches to pick up this unprecedented hope for the peoples of the earth and to carry it as a sacred trust as part of their task of cherishing and protecting "the lives of men and the life of the world" is paralleled by another ethical dilemma: the desire to exploit technical assistance, to make feeding and teaching and curing people into a bribe, to keep the peoples of other countries on our side against Communism. Over and over again one hears the argument that technical assistance is good policy, is the only way to hold back the march of Communism. This is an appropriate argument in the mouths of those who believe that other men will do good deeds only for their own ends, and is of a piece with setting up school lunch programs, not to feed children, but to dispose of surplus agricultural products. Surely, holding back the tide of Communism—or, put in religious terms, fighting the Devil—is a lesser good than cherishing God's children. How can we pause in a discussion of how, if we will, we can bring relief from hunger and pain and ignorance to millions, to suggest that it is also sound national policy? The invocation of this lesser good somehow dims and detracts from the shining purpose with which the vision of what can be done today should be able to infuse the imagination of contemporary Christians. Today there is the possibility of food enough to feed all of his lambs; he said, "heal the sick," and with aureomycin and sulfa, malarial control, immunization and vaccines, "they can be healed." Instead of this vision of a Christian ethic of the brotherhood of man, which is realizable here on earth, now—we have "technical assistance as a useful adjunct of national policy," suitably combined in small proportions with bilateral agreements involving the instruments of warfare. This produces an ethical misalliance between defensive warfare—which can never be defined by religious people as anything but an evil that may nevertheless be absolutely necessary if the conditions which are necessary for religion are not to disappear from the earth—and sharing life and hope between the technically advanced and the technically unadvanced peoples of the world. When technical assistance is thus reduced either to an instrument of anticommunism or to an instrument of purely national policy, it no longer can completely command the religious imaginations of men.

In discussions of Point Four* it was customary and relevant to point out that many of the issues involved were already familiar to Americans who had given willingly of their substance and their lives to bring the Gospel, medicine, education,

*United States bilateral aid policy.

and food to the peoples of other countries. But they have not done this as Americans, but American Christians, as particular groups of Christians, Methodists, or members of the Society of Friends, Episcopalians or Baptists. Even in secular activities of sending food and clothing abroad, Americans have traditionally been extremely generous as individuals or members of voluntary organizations, but grudging and stipulating when it came to Congressional action for the same ends. European observers have often been confused by the apparent paradox of Americans who, in response to an appeal for voluntary abstention from essential foods, responded so magnificently in World War I and who, in World War II, expressed continuous anxiety for fear we would "starve to death" if we tried to feed the world. Yet the difference is quite explicable. I remember discussing this with a British high official abroad during the war, who said, "Anyway, you Americans are not going to export the food that is needed. You are going to eat it up yourselves." When I objected vigorously that the American people had shown over and over again their generosity, their willingness to give up butter and sugar that others might not starve, that, because in this war it was government planned, people had not understood the need, he said, "Go home, and find a religious leader who will be willing to make the people understand." But there was no such religious leader ready; the groups who tried to make Americans realize that a decision not to ration soap would be translated into nutritional deprivation for millions of children were led by left-wing groups with suspect motivations. The actual enormous contribution—which should still have been much greater—that the United States Government made to feeding the world was virtually without benefit of clergy, and loomed in the minds of the American people, not as too little —which they would have considered it had they acted privately and voluntarily, as Christians, rather than as Federal taxpayers —but as too much.

Our ambivalence, as Americans, about the role of the Federal Government, at home and abroad, is a compound of our dislike of the Federal Government getting into habits of playing Santa Claus, and our dislike of anyone receiving handouts. The genius of the Point Four program was that it emphasized the role of Americans, acting through the Federal Government, in providing "know-how" rather than goods, in helping other peoples to help themselves. As such, there was much in the Point Four program which caught the imagination and enlisted the devotion of Americans—as Americans, and as Christians. If there were no other way in which technical assistance could be brought to Iran or Indonesia, then Point Four would represent one of our highest possible aspirations, perhaps exceeding in dramatic if not in real value the activities of voluntary associations of Americans, because the United States Point Four program had to operate in a world where national states took on either the true aspects of the bellwether of the flock, or that of wolves in sheep's clothing.

But Point Four operations were not our best invention because we had already conceived and designed an even better way, and a way that is more congruent with the practice of the brotherhood of man. In giving technical assistance today, and helping other peoples overcome starvation, ignorance, and preventable disease, we have the choice of acting bilaterally, as members of a single, very rich, very prosperous, generous, but necessarily self-interested (for it is the function of national governments to protect their own people against all others) nation-state, or as members of an associated group of nations, in which we who wish to help, and they who need help, meet in an equality of interest and dignity. If Christian generosity and Christian giving are to be congruent with those democratic institutions which visions of the brotherhood of man under the fatherhood of God have done so much to foster, then any discrepancy between giver and receiver which can be wiped out, must be wiped out. Simple sharing, not lordly benefaction, ennobles both giver and receiver while the least extra, unnecessary, in a sense technological discrepancy, begrimes and demeans such sharing.

Within the framework of the United Nations Technical Assistance program, all the members—the United States, Venezuela, France, Indonesia, Norway, although some are larger and stronger, some highly developed technically, some beginners in the task of putting modern science at the service of their peoples—act on a basis of equality within an organization which is their own. When the government of Venezuela or Greece asks help from the United Nations Technical Assistance program, it is one member of a group of brothers asking help from their own group, not the poor asking the rich, or the weak the strong, or the unskilled the technically trained. The United Nations may have to recruit all of the technicians from the highly developed countries, but within international team-frameworks these men will work—in dignified guaranteed equal status—with the representatives of the countries that have asked for assistance. As the richest country the United States may foot the largest bill, not as a single benefactor of the mendicant peoples but as one among the peoples of the world.

Assistance, if stated as a way in which we, the fortunate, may help those less fortunate, has high ethical appeal in focusing the moral energy of Americans, as citizens, on the responsibility of the United States in the modern world. But as Kipling emphasized long ago in his much misunderstood poem, "The White Man's Burden," the task of the more technically developed country—the country whose technology, or religion, or political institutions bear the marks of generations of high-level concerted felicitous effort—is to make the recipients of help not into sycophants or dependents, but into peers, and it is the stated aim that the peoples of Trust Territories be helped to become full self-governing peoples also. Here there need be no confusion between Christian sharing and more limited national interest, no puffed-up pride of superior nation status. The people of any nation who proclaim themselves Christian have a role in regard to other nations in which no incompatible or partial aim need confuse the full involvement of their religious dedication.

But—even granted the more complete suitability of United Nations Technical Assistance progress as the structural expression of the brotherhood of man under the fatherhood of God, where no brother should set himself up above another—we are still in difficulty. We still have with us Christian ambivalence about the fruits of the machine, Christians' willingness to brand (as I have heard it branded by men in holy orders) the desire of mothers that their babies should not die, as "materialism," Christians' willingness to denounce the machine—which as the successor of plow, sickle, and mortar has made it possible for men to live more worthily of their humanity—as the enemy of spirituality. Under an elaborate superstructure which sometimes also draws help from the specious argument that people's cultures should be respected—an argument which got short-enough shrift when it was a matter of giving other people the full details of our culture-laden religious ideas—too many Christians have drawn aside their skirts from the "materialism" of a program that will teach the hungry how to feed themselves, continuing to support the Christian virtues of compassion and resignation, appropriate to the inevitable sufferings of man, in a context of the twentieth century, in which hunger and ignorance and epidemic disease are no longer inevitable, but definitely, immediately preventable.

The religiously gifted knew, centuries early, what men pray for for other men, and I should like to quote from an old Elizabethan prayer:

They that are snared and entangled in the utter lack of things needful for the body cannot set their minds upon Thee as they ought to do; but when they are deprived of the things which they so greatly desire, their hearts are cast down and quail for grief. Have pity upon them, therefore, most merciful Father, and relieve their misery through Thy incredible riches, that, removing their urgent necessity, they may rise up to Thee in mind.

Thou, O Lord, providest enough for all men with Thy most bountiful hand. . . . Give meat to the hungry and drink to the thirsty; comfort the sorrowful, cheer the dismayed and strengthen the weak; deliver the oppressed and give hope and courage to them that are out of heart.

Have mercy, O Lord, upon all forestallers, and upon all them that seek undue profits or unlawful gains. Turn Thou the hearts of them that live by cunning rather than by labour. Teach us that we stand daily and wholly in need of one another. And give us grace, in hand and mind, to add our proper share to the common stock; through Jesus Christ our Lord.

IV Cultural Man
(1966)

Anthropology brings to our knowledge of human beings the
results of several specific kinds of research. This knowledge, in
turn, broadens and deepens our understanding of man as one
among all the living creatures inhabiting this planet in this solar
system. Some anthropological research reaches back millions of
years in time to place man in the context of evolving living
creatures and to trace the evolution of man's various organs and
the development of his capacity to perceive, to organize, to
question, and to begin to understand the universe in which he
lives. By a comparative study of the many forms of culture
which have existed in the past—studied reconstruction of fossil
and archeological remains, of language and other aspects of
culture and surviving living forms—and by direct field observation of behavior and analysis of currently used symbolic forms,
anthropology explores the range of man's capacity to build cultural systems. As a result of the comparative and historical studies which have been conducted during the last century and a
half, two earlier theories about human history have been called
into question. Although our present knowledge leaves no doubt

that social forms have gone through large-scale evolutionary changes, in which simple food gathering and hunting have been succeeded by agriculture and animal husbandry and that these in turn have developed into man's present industrial and technical control of nature today, the nineteenth-century assumption that all other forms of culture—man's artistic, intellectual, social, and religious life—were tied to this evolution of technical culture is no longer tenable. Detailed work has revealed a tremendous variety of cultural behavior, with complexity of symbolic forms often associated with simplicity of technical or social organization. It has also called in question the latter assumption, made so often by social commentators who claim to base their statements on anthropological and sociological evidence, that the process of urbanization results in some kind of deterioration in human behavior. Against this assumption they would place the material that shows that small isolated human communities may also represent profound deterioration in human relationships—the peoples of the Baliem valley the Mundugumor of the Yuat River in New Guinea, the isolated peoples of the mountains in many Euro-American communities—and that the deterioration which results from urbanization is a function of transition and of ensuing social disorganization, and not of the process of civilization itself. Though not exalting the present state of our own culture to a position of absolute improvement over all preceding cultures, modern anthropological evolutionary theory recognizes the correlates of technical advances in man's increasing capacity for communication, for organization into larger and larger communities of individuals all defined as members of one group and for greater understanding, and the resulting enlargement of possibilities of effective ordering of human social behavior. As a correlate of this extension of our knowledge of the particular steps by which man has developed to his present physical, cultural, and social condition, anthropology is also concerned with possible future change. We know that man's body and physical capacities have responded to long-time changes in the conditions of life, as men acquired and elaborated on the ability to grow, store, and prepare food; the ability to provide shelter and clothing as protections against inclement weather; the ability to work with and transform the earth's natural resources, creating implements and machines and new sources of energy and even new kinds of raw materials; the ability to record and transmit—at a distance and to future generations—much that men have experienced; and the ability to organize themselves into even larger and more complex communities, especially as they acquired new and increasingly rapid forms of communication and transportation.

It is, therefore, also the task of anthropology to consider the possible future development of man under new conditions: great density of population, the burden of the knowledge of how to bring about a catastrophe in which not only warring groups but all mankind and perhaps all living creatures might be destroyed, the possibilities inherent in the new technologies. In the distant past inventions like the wheel, the sail, the plow, and the loom increased men's simple mastery over their external environment. In today's technology machines have been substituted not only for the most complex manual tasks, but even for every complex activity of discrimination, memory, and decision—tasks which once were performed by the human brain without external aids, just as men once tilled the soil with nothing but digging sticks in their hands.

A Wider Perspective on Mankind

This, then, is the first contribution that anthropological thought can make to Christian thinking: an increasingly detailed and concrete specification of the steps by which man has attained his present physical, cultural, and social state; a growing recognition of that state as itself a changing one; and, because of man's newly acquired ability to understand his own past and present, a growing awareness that man's state is increasingly coming under his own control, be it for good or for evil.

Traditionally, as men relied on the concrete terms in which the Scriptures were cast by their writers, men whose inspiration was informed and shaped by their location in time and space, the sense of man as a changing creature, living in a world which man himself was altering, was little emphasized. Biblical parallels to urbanization might be sought in the fall of Sodom and Gomorrah, and the plowshare and the pruning hook were likely to be treated as if they had been placed in man's hand at the gate of the Garden. For men whose widest knowledge of the world extended to parts of Asia and Europe—for whom most of Africa and all of the Americas and Australia were beyond the widest stretch of the imagination—the constricted nature of the ancient world was accepted as a kind of prototype of civilization. Men might temporarily progress. They might build great cities, wage great wars, and carry out great enterprises. But then a great civilization would collapse and fall back again, apparently without intrinsic change, into broken and lesser versions of the past, as the tower of Babel, which men in their temerity attempted to build, collapsed into ruin.

Anthropological research also introduces questions about the possibilities and the limitations inherent in man's physical being, as expressive of the paths he has trodden, and a wider consideration of human perception and the kinds of human social organization—and, therefore, of human communities—which have existed, do exist, and may exist in the future on this planet.

Perhaps the simplest way of stating this is to emphasize that our view of man today must include men who lived half a million years ago, men who had only the crudest and simplest of tools and the most rudimentary forms of social organization, and, equally, men living today who represent technical stages not unlike theirs, who still can be found living in remote parts of the earth, whose traditions are as old as ours but far simpler than the traditional way of life of the Hebrew people at the beginning of their recorded history. Underwriting the Christian extrapolation to all men of man made in the image of God and man within whom Christ can be perceived, there is now the detailed accumulation of research materials on fossil man, ancient man, and primitive man—materials which make possible a general outline of human history as the history of a species. And this species, like other species, can be described as one, that is, as a living group in which even the most remotely separated individuals in space can, if they are brought together, mate and have offspring. But in addition to these characteristics which men share with other related species and with some species very far removed in the evolutionary scale—for example, care by both parents, the importance of vision and uprightness are shared with birds—men have depended on a human ability to develop into persons within the setting provided by the group, yet responsive to the individuality of each. Underwriting the biblical admonition to love one's neighbor is our knowledge of the many thousands of ways in which small groups of men have struggled toward wider conceptions of neighborliness. Underwriting the Christian insistence on the unending nature of man's struggle on earth to reconcile his natural impulses with Christian ideals of conduct, there is the long record of the struggles of human societies, sometimes succeeding and sometimes failing, to develop a social order within which men could follow Christian admonitions. Comparative studies also reveal the perennial struggle in every society to rear children and support adult individuals so that the ideal of the good life, however differently defined, may triumph over man's conflictual tendencies toward good and evil.

Modern anthropology also places in a new context the problems which arise from a belief in inevitable progress and those which arise from a belief in man's essentially unending battle between his original nature and his aspirations. During the nineteenth century and into the first years of the twentieth, the difficulties encountered in reading the fossil records, on the one hand, and the continuing ethnocentrism of Euro-Americans, on the other, had as one result the tendency to treat evolution, the progressive transformation of biological forms through time, and social progress as in some sense interchangeable concepts, leaving little room for the eternal nature of the struggle as seen by the Christian. But modern anthropology, following the lead of modern biology, broke away from the simple notion that all biological evolution is in and of itself progressive; and the accumulating record of early cultures freed our thought from the ethnocentrism which underlies the assumption that all civilization originated in Asia. The elaboration of the many ways in which biological specialization, on the one hand, and cultural forms of learned behavior, on the other, can become blind alleys—or can be lost—increases our understanding of the ephemeral and fragile character of man's present and past. It also clarifies man's future temporal-spatial relationships both to the rest of the biological world and to the societies he builds, within which he must live. Thus modern cultural anthropology and modern biological theory have summarily resolved the conflict between Christian ideas of the person and nineteenth-century conceptions of man which developed out of that century's very partial understanding of man, in his temporal and spatial extent, millions of years back in time, spread over the entire globe and living at very different technical and social levels.

Modern anthropological theory provides a scientific background for the acceptance of man as part of the living world of God's creatures, for our creatureliness and for continuity within the whole creation. It provides a scientific basis for man's view of himself, in spite of all the differences among various localized races and physical stocks, as one species and for the relevance of a spiritual message to all men, regardless of their historical or spatial relationship to the Hebraic, Greco-Roman, and Euro-American traditions. And it supports the recognition that the entire sociocultural framework of human life—including the forms of the family, the organization of the community, and the techniques of survival, travel, and communication—is historically dependent on specific cultural conditions. So man may, through the civilizations that he builds, advance or regress or even threaten the existence of his own species.

Within this wider perspective on mankind many of the barriers to the ecumenical movement crumble away. Great civilizations which arose outside the specific tradition within which the Judeo-Christian sequence came into being need not be equated with barbarism. The relative readiness of members of different races and different societies to assume the full burden of ministry need not be attributed to race or to some conception of "higher" or "lower" levels of civilization which itself suggests the natural superiority or inferiority of some groups of men to others. Change of all kinds can be recognized and accepted as inherent in the historical process through which men have become what they are and without which human society would not flower but would stagnate. Some particular period in the past need no longer be artificially deified into a period of virtue, stability, and harmony with God's will. The written word can be seen as *one* historically developed form of recorded inspiration. And no one vehicle of communication—through script or oral communication, dramatic ritual, radio, television, or communications satellite—need be treated as somehow more divinely inspired or blessed than any other. There need be no opposition between simple and "natural" ways of life—tilling the soil, planting the vineyard, or shepherding the flock—and the fabrication of goods by machines, between walking and traveling by train or car or jet plane, between laboriously pre- paring a concordance of the Scriptures by hand and using a computer. Repudiation of the machine can be seen as the local response of men at a particular time and place when machines were first and with great difficulty being incorporated into the sociocultural life of the community. It can be regarded as one response to sociocultural dislocation, not as being due to any inherent opposition between the religiously blessed life and secular or satanic versions of life.

In earlier anthropological work the delineation of concrete behaviors which were thought of as good and as evil by the members of particular cultures served as one means of stressing the contrast between different societies and cultures. This stress on concretely different views of good and evil often seemed to those who approached the problems of Christian ethics to pro- mote a sterile relativism and to remove any scientific basis in the study of man for the recognition of universals. This interpre- tation of anthropological findings failed to take fully into ac- count the interconnectedness of culture—a failure in which some anthropologists also shared. The statement that in a cer- tain society elders were permitted to choose their own death rather than endanger the survival of their grandchildren, and that their children were bound to assist them in this purpose, or the statement that in a particular society marriage was en- joined with one kind of first cousin or, in special cases, was enjoined with a sibling, seemed, to some, to indicate the ab- sence of any scientific basis for universal ethical restraints on murder or incest—or even the absence of any scientific basis for legal restraints.

The present position in anthropology emphasizes the univer- sality of an ethical sense as part of man's inherent human capac- ities; and anthropologists agree with the biologists who have identified the role played in human evolution by the capacity to accept from trusted elders a standard of behavior. Thus the natural order, scientifically explored, provides, as at present understood, no basis for the sterile relativism which so recently was seen (and residually is seen) as a scientifically based position in opposition to that taken in Christian ethics.

Exploration of the forms that man's imagination takes—even in the simplest primitive societies, untouched by contact with culture-transcending religion—suggests that there may be a biological basis in man, and in man alone, for the capacity to relate to the universe—which has been called the sense of wonder or the cosmological or cosmic sense. This would involve recognition that biological evolution includes not only the extension, elaboration, and specialization of biological capacities found in prehominid species, but that there may be specifically human, biological needs which are an intrinsic part of man's search for God. The need to make the perceived universe meaningful and coherent, to each individual person, to apprehend and in some measure re-create the universe may be likened to a need as biological as the need for oxygen, for water, for food, and for rest—a need that is not denied in any human being without consequences.

The Transcendency of Christian Culture

Comparative anthropological studies of cultures in different parts of the world, at different levels of technological development, complex as well as primitive, have led to the recognition that no item of culture is carried in the genes. Each individual is dependent on learning to become a full human being—a person who speaks a language, shares with his fellows a view of other human beings, has acquired techniques for sustaining life, and relates himself and all men to the universe. Once this is recognized, it is clear that no aspect of any culture is irrelevant to the Christian ideal of man in community with his fellowmen. Each facet is crucial—the relation between men and tools and machines, the development of political organizations within which men, with however much difficulty, live at peace with one another, the development of forms of communication which make it possible for those of like mind to share their vision of God in a world of accelerating change. And, to the extent that men are called upon to live in accordance with the Pauline definition, "we are members one of another" (Eph. 4:25), no ground plan of the church militant can afford to ignore these findings.

Like all men, the man who dedicates himself to the Christian way of life has been reared in a particular society. Like all men, he has, in the course of his upbringing, become a human being, capable of understanding what he hears and sees and of conducting his life with others. But to the extent that the culture in which he has been reared is in some ways lacking—is able to integrate only a few individuals within a common membership; is weak in the authority necessary for the maintenance of peace and order; is deficient in the production of food and goods and lacking in devices for sharing them equitably among its members; is clumsy in handling the growing child's perception of the world; or is deficient in the expression of the brotherhood of man—to this extent is his ability to lead a Christian life impaired. However diverse the requirements may be—from the ability to accept guidance in matters of ethical choice, the capacity to treat sex relations as a responsibility, the ability to read, the ability to learn foreign languages (often an unrecognized demand that churches make upon new converts), the ability to accept stewardship, to the ability to appreciate the finest points of the Christian ethical concept of a personal relationship to God—the requirements themselves, the individual's view of them and his ability to fulfill them depend on the culture within which he has been reared or which he has accepted as a learning individual, accepting full membership.

The history of Christianity has been a history of continual

reinterpretation of the Old and New Testaments in terms of particular cultures and periods. Over and over again the revelations of the Scriptures have been clothed and reshaped by the language and the imagery, the minutiae of the local social scene, the local forms of family, community, and national social organization. The fate of Christian understanding has been a very different one, depending on the cultural context on which it is embedded. Very different aspects of belief have been emphasized and elaborated in cultures with strong patriarchal or monarchical institutions and in cultures with bilateral systems of family organization or more egalitarian, democratic institutions.

In the past this diversity of forms has been used, quite appropriately, to stress the universality of the Christian message. It demonstrated that a message from a God of all men, speaking to all men, could cross every barrier and defy any frontier and could be embodied in the poetry and the artistic forms of any group of men. Cultures were diverse, but Christian culture could become universal. The preaching of the gospel in Japanese and Bantu, in Hawaiian and Gaelic, in Italian and Swahili, was in itself a tribute to its universality.

Historically, however, this emphasis on the transcendency of Christian culture has been compromised in several ways. It has been implicitly assumed, for example, that the language and imagery of Hebrew, Greek, and Latin (and, later, English, German, and French) are somehow closer to God's purpose than the languages and imagery of peoples who are not the descendants, direct or indirect, of the writers of the Old and New Testaments. From this it followed that members of other cultures could understand the Christian message only if their own basic imagery were altered. The demand for change has taken many forms—sometimes explicitly expressed and sometimes only implicit in some set of rules or expectations. So it is sometimes demanded that converts learn the languages of the seminaries and the languages in which commentaries have been written. Or it may be insisted that trousers for men and skirts for women are somehow more "Christian" than skirts for men and trousers for women, or that sex distinction in dress is essential to the Christian life or that a given number of meals a day —as well as food to sustain life—is intrinsic to God's purposes.

The anthropological approach introduces here a double consideration. As human behavior is always viewed in context, no detail of language or dress or political organization can be seen as intrinsic to a religion which explicitly states that its mission is to all men. Thus anthropological analysis would support the effort to strip Christianity of culturally limiting elements in the language of worship, the form and the materials of the church building, and the character of the church polity.

But the same approach leads anthropology also to recognize that Christianity is a historical movement, localized in time and space, historically cast in a certain mold, embodied in the imagery and the vision of a particular group of prophets and saints, and brought to its present state as a culture through centuries in which its primary relationships have been with the cultures of Europe and the Near East, not the cultures of Asia or southern Africa, Australia, or the Americas. A message of the depth and complexity of the Christian message can be communicated from one human being to another and from one generation to another only through the medium of a particular language, a particular set of social forms, a particular set of images. Therefore, in recognizing both that these are historically given and that the Christian message is applicable to all men, whatever language they speak, whatever historical tradition they may share, whatever their level of technical advancement may be, it is important also to recognize that a process of cultural transformation occurs as the message is received and transmitted in different cultures. Then the humanity conferred by the local culture becomes the foundation for a wider understanding of total Christian culture, as it has been enriched and elaborated, pruned and shaped by men of different cultures, all of whom share its great culture-transcending tradition.

An anthropological understanding of culture provides not only an appreciation of how members of each generation in a particular society are enculturated in their local language, community, and nation, but also of the systematic interrelationships and interdependencies within larger cultural units—of which Christianity among other world religions is one. Thus the futile struggle to create a kind of historical situation in which all non-Christian cultures are equated, regardless of their level of civilization, is replaced by a recognition of Christianity as a culture that transcends local cultures, comparable in this respect to Buddhism or Islam or modern Communism—each of which also has developed a culture-transcending system which crosses the bounds of local cultures and can be learned by men of many different cultural backgrounds. The special nature of Christian truth and Christian revelation is not involved or compromised by such a recognition. Rather, Christianity is seen as a system which in some matters overlaps with other great religions and ideologies, but which is unique in its total configuration and which presents mutually exclusive choices to those who profess to be Christians instead of members of some other worldwide system.

The anthropological approach to the study of man has led to an understanding of man as becoming human within the culture in which he is reared and to the recognition that the purely human values of any one culture should not be elevated above those of any other. But it would also support the proposition that the Christian church itself represents a culture into which individuals may be born or which they may enter (or leave), the versions of which may have a more or less systematic relationship to one another at any historical period.

From this viewpoint, strain within the church occurs as the

Christian community feels and responds to change within other parts of a constituent culture-change which may be expressed through technology, scientific knowledge, political organization, or new conceptions of man's relationship to man. As the Christian church is almost never coextensive with the whole of the culture of any society within which it exists, there is inevitably a tension between changes in values in those parts of the culture which have a different focus—for example, technical or scientific innovation, taxation, trade unionism—and the desire for the conservation of values in the Christian tradition. Particularly in the modern world, as an accelerating consciousness of social change has led to a sharpening of ethical issues, this tension has increased and the positions taken by the various Christian churches have become less well articulated.

Seen from an anthropological viewpoint, the ecumenical movement can be interpreted as a way of dealing with those historical inconsistencies and discrepancies, as the attempt is made to arrive at a new community of understanding among churches with very different conceptions of their responsibilities in regard to the quality of the relationships of widely separated peoples, the mounting pressure of world population, the crucial necessity of developing new methods of conflict resolution, and the care, protection, and education of those who stand in need in the worldwide community.

In the early days of the Christian church, language—Latin in western Europe and Greek in eastern Europe—served as an integrating mechanism, drawing together a whole part of the Christian world. Today the common effort to relate Christian theology and Christian ethics to the findings of science, the growth of technology, the changing size and form of political units and emerging ideas of social responsibility also can become a unifying mechanism. With such a focusing of attention at the higher level of the culture-transcendent Christian community, the kinds of problems which have been worked out in some Christian communities but not in others—concern about evolution or machines or supranational organizations or the welfare state—will be seen not as barriers, but as removable stumbling blocks. Furthermore, as we have come to understand the importance of social structure in permitting or preventing or promoting more inclusive and sensitive human relationships, it has been recognized that changes in the organization of relationships—such as changes in forms of association, in residential patterns, in the worker's relationship to his job, in the communication of contrasting forms of behavior associated with national, ethnic, or class differences—can go far toward reconciling groups once in conflict. The comparative study of different cultural forms gives us access to a variety of forms of reconciliation and also a knowledge of destructive possibilities against which we must be watchful as we realize that any type of behavior which is found institutionalized in any human culture must be regarded as sufficiently human as to be capable of becoming actualized in any other culture.

Within the wider context it will be apparent that many controversies about the Christian role in determining the type of community which the larger society should choose and maintain are reconcilable. Differences among men which are essentially the products of social history—differences based on ancestry, rank, caste, class, or race—will be recognized as irrelevant to the Christian view of man. (For the Christian member of a Western society, looking at caste in Hindu society, this is an obvious conclusion.) Similarly, any exclusiveness of community which draws on such historical differences will be recognized as contrary to the Christian conception of man's relationship to man. There is no basis, other than the historical one represented in local cultures, for separation at worship, exclusion from the ministry, or prohibitions on marriage or on any forms of social, political, and economic equality because of membership in one physical stock rather than another.

Anthropological research can give no support to the belief that any particular form of division of labor, any one set of rules for fixing social status by age or sex or race, any inalienable attachment to the land is an embodiment of God's laws. Clearly, all such practices have changed through time and vary in different cultures; and in their different forms all have been looked upon as according with Christian principles. Ideas about the use of money, usury or interest, just payment and credit—all of which have from time to time become interwoven with the prohibitions and admonitions of Christian communities—are equally the products of social history, subject to change and open to examination, within a given context, for the extent to which they enable men, within that context, to come closer to God.

The refusal to make use of the possibilities of the modern world—the refusal to use technology, to fit a church with a loudspeaker, to permit an eye-graft that will preserve sight or a blood transfusion that may preserve life, the refusal to travel by plane or to use new materials for ritual garments—all these things, mere stumbling blocks as they may be, reduce the capacity of the Christian church to be a time-binding and a culture-transcending institution.

No single institution as such is more Christian than another. For those who are concerned with the problem of the Christian community and the congruence of institutions within Christian culture, it is necessary to raise the discussion to a higher level. We may then appropriately ask: At a given time and in a given place, within the sense of ethics and the economics of possibility, which kinds of institutions, organized in relationship to each other—international, national, local, concerned with work, with men's formal and informal relations and with the life of the family—best provide for the life of men together, through which men may become more human and better able to relate themselves to God?

New Areas of Integration

The technical-functional view of man is, in the eyes of some theologians, opposed to the personal-cultural view of man. However, it can be better understood as a response to new organizations in an emerging world society, with larger populations, larger units of organization, greater interchangeability of roles, higher rates of lateral and vertical mobility, and far more inclusive systems of communication.

The close-knit relationship between parent and child, teacher and child, and child in the church, which, even in the recent past, provided for an almost complete integration of what was taught, learned, and experienced, has been altered by relationships with far greater diversity and spread. Marriages take place between individuals who differ profoundly in culture and belief. Schools are taught by teachers whose backgrounds and life are exceedingly diverse. The child's relationship to the church is only one of the multiple relationships to sources of authority and leadership.

In most parts of today's changing world there is a search for new kinds of integration of different aspects of life. In some of the most socially mobile parts of the world, as in the United States of America, it is the church which can provide new areas of integration as all members of the family may be part of the church's extended social milieu. At the same time, the newly recognized obligation of the church to play an active role in breaking down class, race, and ethnic barriers gives special weight to the demand on the church to be receptive and inclusive, not to sacrifice this mission to the wider world in the interests of a narrower and superficially more spiritually comforting like-mindedness. And these two functions of the modern church—to provide a center of like-mindedness and to welcome and comfort the stranger within the community gates —are everywhere called into play as people move from primitive life to peasant life, from peasant life to urban life, from one region of a country to another, and from nation to nation, sometimes willingly, as immigrants, and sometimes under pressure, as refugees.

Certain of the necessary adjustments will be made more easily if, instead of concentrating narrowly on the present, a deeper and broader time perspective is invoked. That is, we can enlarge our sense of what is possible to the extent that we look at questions of inclusiveness and exclusiveness (the breadth of communion which should be sought; the depth of the hold which the religious community, within the wider community, should have on the child) within the widest framework, placing the growth of Christianity within the perspective of the growth of all religions.

It is necessary to realize that throughout man's history there have been periods and occasions, even in very primitive communities, when sudden and intense inspirational emphases have resulted in attempts to form totalistic communities. In a community of this kind every detail of life is made subject to a particular religious rule. Over time some of these attempts have shrunk, fragmented, and died; others have diffused and have been reabsorbed into the wider stream of life; and still others have become the foundation for what may be called a church which exists within and as part of a wide community.

Occurring particularly during periods of change and transition, the totalistic approach to the religious life—whether it takes the form of individual retreat into isolation, as in the case of the hermit, or that of the ascetic community, or that of the economically self-contained cult—is, in these circumstances, an almost predictable expression of renewed inspiration and of the struggle to achieve a more integrated approach to the universe. There is, of course, a difference in scale between the small cults that spring up by the thousand among primitive people in parts of the world which have been more recently penetrated, the religious orders that have been formed during periods of social disorganization or even chaos, the quietist cults that developed during the Reformation, the utopian communities that came into being in response to the ideas of the Enlightenment, and the types of political integration that we have designated as "totalitarian." But in certain respects they are all similar in kind. Any facet of life can temporarily be regarded as having an overriding value which should take precedence over every other consideration in life and in terms of which the whole of life should be organized.

But significantly, in the long history of man, those religious and political philosophies have survived which have been capable of providing inspiration and leadership in a thousand diverse contexts—which have been meaningful to rich and poor, the possessors and the dispossessed and disinherited, the landowner and the landless, the healthy and the sick, the intelligent and the simple-minded, the intellectual and the craftsman.

It is understandable that in the world today there should be, within the Christian church, movements toward each of these two kinds of inclusiveness. It is understandable that there should be a movement toward withdrawal from the world into a totalistic way of life in which each detail of work and worship, each detail of companionship and solitude, each thought that is allowed to pass through the brain, is minutely regulated in terms of some special vision of a close, exclusive, and all-exacting relationship to God. It is equally understandable that there should be a complementary struggle to widen the tenets of Christianity, guarding against the possibility that Christianity might become the religion of one race, one part of the world, one political or economic system, and strengthening the assurance that as the scientific and technological sectors of culture increase the number and kinds of contacts between all societies, the church will be able to speak to them all.

The recognition that total withdrawal of the faithful, on the one hand, and far-reaching spiritual participation in the intellectual heritage of the modern world, on the other, are both responses to the consciousness of change in the world and to the fact that each has a long history—sometimes productive, sometimes deadening—as a response to change, can do much to prevent an unnecessary cleavage. For, however different, these are related responses to change. There is no basis for arguing, for example, that those who advocate withdrawal into the religious life or into a total religious community must necessarily be the advocates of conservatism and obscurantism and that only those who stand for full Christian participation in the world today should be regarded as modern, contemporary-minded, future-oriented, and intellectually and scientifically sophisticated.

It should be recognized, in fact, that this particular division between conservation and innovation, taken as a whole, represents only one of the many lines of tension between religious concentration and religious diffusion. Many other combinations are possible. Totalistic sects may well embrace modern technology. Religious orders may work concentratedly on modern biological research. Those who have put distance between themselves and mundane cares may do far the best work in restoring the physically handicapped through the most modern prosthetics.

The World Council of Churches can draw upon the widest possible range of Christian forms; among its members there are new cults, old orders, wise old churches, and energetic revivified older religious communities. One of the functions of the Council may well be to prevent the occurrence of single lines of cleavage on the issue of the mission of the Christian church to the world and to reidentify the contributions which can be made by those who withdraw to work or to pray with the contributions which are made by those whose work lies in the world, as these different groups may become in a wider sense the conscience of the Christian world.

In the Midst of Time

The contribution of anthropology lies principally in providing a longer time perspective and a wider context for the consideration of the problem of the Christian as person in community. By placing man in his long evolutionary history, anthropological research can help to correct the limited and limiting image of man as the user of simple agricultural tools who, when the machine loom and the steam engine were invented, was betrayed into worldliness and removed from the labor decreed by God; as the simple reader of the Bible whose piety has been corrupted by radio and television; as properly the inhabitant of the small, hierarchical community in which each person had a hereditary place, whose sense of right order has been corrupted and lost as a result of migration and urbanization; as the simple stargazer who saw God's perfection in the starry firmament and who was driven to doubt and disbelief by the new vision of the universe made possible by the telescope; as the believer who, identifying sumptuary laws and dietary practices and the eschewal of small pleasures with the will of God, is corrupted by a wider perspective on human morals. Anthropology can help us to recognize, instead, that all these have been—and are—temporary expressions of a deeper human ethic which, to be meaningful, must strive toward the universal.

This sense of perspective illumines and revises the images of historic man so that it is possible to appreciate man's tremendous struggle, in his dawning humanity, to make the world a place in which new generations of men and their children could live more safely and more fully, more wisely and more meaningfully. This in turn makes it possible to recognize that today's world, with its enormous, intercommunicating population, its burgeoning technology, and its newly aroused consciousness and conscience, is not the evil and corrupt end of a historical epoch, but, rather, represents one stage on a long, long journey —a far longer journey than the majority of Christians have imagined.

Each stage—each step—on this journey not only is marked by technical mastery over some aspect of the environment which man has accomplished by effort (the real meaning of "work"; for animals do not alter their environment, they merely live within it); it is also characterized by the widening of human horizons which accompanies technical change. Within this per- spective, agriculture (a very late human invention) ceases to be the prototype of life on emergence from the Garden. Instead, we see a human creature, frail and almost defenseless against other creatures, equipped only with the capacity to know good and evil and the capacity to shape his evnironment—to invent tools and weapons, shelter and clothing, institutions and laws— as his special resources in the struggle for survival. By including the thousands of years before the invention of gardening (the simplest sowing and harvesting and keeping of seeds for an- other season) and herding (the simplest gathering in of animals and guarding their young), the whole of our perspective on more recent history alters. It becomes easier to plan the rise of town and urban settlements, when food which was planted and stored was sufficient to feed large numbers of people, and the beginnings of trade and communication, as men ventured across the land and down the rivers and even out of sight of land on the seas. And so it becomes easier also to visualize our life today as part of man's long history, presenting new complexi- ties, but complexities that are no less open to comprehension and mastery than those that followed earlier innovations.

In this larger context it is apparent that it is as human to invent and use a computer as it was to invent and use an abacus, and as human to invent and use an electric clock as it was to invent and follow the moving shadow of a sun clock. This opening up of the past allows us also to look forward to a future as far removed from the present as we today are removed from the time when men had as their only tool a chipped stone ax.

But this accomplishment—this ability to place ourselves in the midst of time—is dependent also on a willingness to revise our view of man, made in the image of God, to include an understanding of man as a temporally emerging, growing, and changing being. It includes the incorporation into our perception of the Christ in all men, a recognition that it is through the very diversity of human culture that the universal in our humanness may be found. And this accomplishment becomes fully meaningful only as we recognize that man, struggling over and over again with the loss of innocence and today possessed of powers almost as dread as those refused by Christ in the wilderness, needs a greater and more vital spiritual vision, not a lesser one, than when men planted vineyards and gathered the grapes in a pastoral community two thousand years ago.

▼ Twentieth Century Faith Must Use Technology
(1966)

How can human beings attain full personhood in relation to God and their fellowmen in the contemporary world? We know this involves: what happens to the child in the family, what happens to the family in the neighborhood, and what happens to men face to face with each other. But a new dimension has been added in recent years.

It is, of course, not entirely new. It has been growing for a long time, growing throughout the Christian centuries in our recognition of what it means to love thy neighbor as thyself. During the ages people knew very few neighbors and had no idea how many people existed on this earth. It is only in the past twenty-five years that we really have known who all our neighbors are, where they are, how many there are. (We are not quite sure just how many there are.)

But substantially our planet has been explored. We know we have just one human species—to reinforce our Christian understanding of who our neighbors are. We know that for the first time in human history all of the human race scattered over the continents of the world are in communication with one another. For the first time in human history the fate of any group is the fate of all of us. For centuries and centuries and throughout the early Christian Era the destruction of all the inhabitants of one continent would have left the human race intact. The Americans were cut off from Europe and Asia, and though we were threatened by dreadful conquests and the Black Death, still the human race itself was safe.

It is only today that the whole human race, all of God's children, are now precariously placed within the human responsibility to care for them. Man faces in America a situation we faced spiritually before, but not in sober fact, of being the keepers of all the people of this earth. No disturbance anywhere, no epidemic anywhere, no famine anywhere is outside our knowledge and outside our responsibility.

Now this means we need new forms of community so our children can learn as little children, and we ourselves can relearn as adults what this community means. We are reaching a breakthrough in a new wave of Christian consciousness of where we are trying to go in the world.

Through the ages the Christian message "thou shalt love thy neighbor as thyself" has meant that Christians shared their food with the hungry. They gave to the poor who came to their doorstep. They bound up the wounds of those who were injured in wars they did not know how to prevent, and they buried the children they did not know how to save.

The measure of what they could do in relation to their Christian command was frightfully small. Very often only by shutting out the knowledge of how many other people were starving over the sea or on the other side of the mountain was it possible to survive at all. The will was there, the faith was there, the message was there, but the means were lacking.

Today we have the means and the technical and scientific knowledge to do the things we have always wanted to do. It is not that the task has changed. It has increased in magnitude.

More than a billion people are hungry. Now we have the knowledge so that neither a single child nor more than a billion people *need* go hungry any longer.

This gives us an opportunity we never had before. The opportunity has to be measured against the Christian response in the nineteenth century, particularly to the first appearances of the technological application of science to human affairs. Most of those first applications were accompanied by terrible human misery. I am speaking generally about the nineteenth century. In the last century there was terrible exploitation in the new factories, in the techniques in the mines, and these are still going on in many parts of the world today.

Those who see this may still see technology as the enemy of man and feel that it is dehumanizing, that it has reduced man to a machine and that we have lost something very valuable. But the new technology, made possible by the scientific discoveries of the last quarter of a century, means that we can now humanize man rather than dehumanize him.

I can use the pearls around my neck as an example. Pearls have always stood for luxury. They were put around the necks of queens and princesses or sewed on vestments when the Church was drawing to itself the riches of the world. But for these pearls not even an oyster gave its life and no human diver —no South Sea Islander exploited by colonialism—risked his life to get these pearls.

Yet they are not fakes—they are made with exactly the same materials. Instead of the oyster doing the work and the human diver risking his life to find them, we now make them synthetically from comparable materials. No hungry man will be tempted to steal them. This I think can be used as a measure of the change that is coming over the world.

Whenever we speak of science and technology and what the new empirical knowledge means for man, we must remember those people to whom it means for the first time light at night.

Do you realize that for a hundred thousand years people had to go to bed and stay there if there was no moon?

Today with light they can read. They can move safely and freely where before they often had to bar their doors because the night and danger were so close together. We have to understand those that say technology is good, it's wonderful, give us more right away! We have to realize how surprised and disgusted those people are to hear others worry about the dehumanization of their children's souls through television.

The people of the world who feel that for the first time children born to them do not have to die and women can face childbearing without fearing death must be brought together with worried citizens of the Western world who say that bringing up children is such a dreadful responsibility nowadays.

As we encounter one another we encounter these differences, and we encounter the question of how we are going to discuss the principal task of Christians in this era. The nature of sin does not change, but the particular sins of particular centuries may change their emphases. Today I think the sin we are in danger of committing, and some people may already have committed it rather heavily, is the sin of failing to use the knowledge that exists.

By knowledge I mean empirical knowledge, the knowledge of how to grow food on an acre of ground so that one man's work can support fifty people instead of three or five—simple, technical, empirical knowledge. This knowledge tells us how to deal with malnutrition, how to care for the health of children, and how to stem the population explosion resulting from the application of our Christian principle of valuing every human life.

If we had not put our emphasis on the value of every human being, we might not have developed our public health measures in preventive medicine. We cured epidemics all over the world, we reduced the infant death rate, and now we have the possibility that every child that is born will live. We also have the responsibility to see that only children who can be fed, cared for, and educated are born. We have created this situation in the world, and we have the knowledge to deal with it. We must use it. If we don't, a situation has been created in the world which may bring famine and misery and death to millions of people.

Technology is here. It has made us one world in interdependence and intercommunication.

I have spent most of my adult life working with people at the very fringe of civilization, with the simplest people that the world knows—the people of New Guinea. These two million people speak seven hundred languages. Among them no one knew how to bind more than five hundred people together in any sort of community at all.

From that point of view I can appreciate how far we have come. We learned first to be a tribe, then a city-state, then a nation, and now seek to build a world society bound together by law. From that point of view, also, I can bring a kind of faith and knowledge of how rapidly a people can change. I have seen a single village where I worked thirty-seven years ago skip about two thousand years since then.

I knew the villagers before they became Christians, when they lived in the Stone Age, when every man had been a headhunter. They had no knowledge of the world beyond their little island. I knew them after their first understanding of Christianity, in which the missionary valued their souls but still treated them as of another order. I knew them after they combined the vision of human brotherhood with a recognition of what modern political forms and modern technology might bring. Then they spoke of the older form of Christianity which they learned from missionaries who had never heard of a well baby clinic (although with great compassion they bound up any wound that came to them).

The task of the Christian community today is to learn to

combine the command to love our neighbors as ourselves with the task of finding out who our neighbors are, knowing all that is known about them and knowing all that can be known about carrying out the Christian command.

This has two general applications. It means the Christian community must demand that the scientist, natural scientist and social scientist put their knowledge in a form so that it can be used by the ordinary human being. There are scientists, quite a few of them, who have tried to do this, but it is a one-sided matter until the Christian community also acts. Man must ask the social sciences—the sciences which know how to organize the international world, how to organize law, how to build administrative sturctures—how to express the love of man to man. We must ask the scientists to tell us what they know today about how to rear little children so they will grow up with the capacity to trust and love God, to feel sin and to relate themselves to the whole of the human race. We know what these conditions are but they are being taken very little account of in many Christian communities in the world.

We know what the conditions are for building the big city, and we are building terrible cities in every part of the world. We know what is necessary for little children, and we are not carrying these principles out. So we need to ask from all the scientists: These are the things we believe need to be done, now tell us what your science can say.

I was horrified when a student said to me that the danger of nuclear warfare is just American propaganda, and I would have been equally horrified if he had said it was Russian propaganda or Chinese propaganda or French propaganda or Guatemalan propaganda. The horrible thing is our inability to recognize that we Americans hold the lives of the whole world in our hands. War, any war, anywhere, endangers the whole world and people of each country now are the keepers of the members of every other country. No country can protect itself. No country anywhere by the bravery of sacrifice or effort of its own citizens can protect itself today—we can only effectively protect our own citizens in any country if we protect all the others also.

If theology can be illuminated by a greater knowledge of the world in which we live, theology will be given a new life in our time. We will not be losing a large proportion of our young people because they feel lonely in an atmosphere that does not take into account what they know. One of the important facts of our time is that because of the rapidity of this social, techno-logical, secularizing, pluralistic world revolution, young people know more than their elders. They have always felt they did—now they do.

They never knew a world without the bomb, the very young-est ones never knew a world without a satellite in the sky. We have to work out some way in which the world where they are natives, and we are immigrants, can be related to the world which belongs to those of us who are older. We not only have the tasks of leadership and authority, we have a sense of ur-gency that the young do not have.

It is absolutely urgent that Christians should take as a first responsibility to know what is known. We do not want to take our depleted ranks and make them all physicists, chemists, or behavioral scientists. We want to ask as citizens—who are also Christians—that the scientists tell us what is known so that we can use this knowledge.

We must take upon ourselves the task of providing a twen-tieth-century faith we can put together with empirical knowl-edge. Theologians must work with scientists to build this new faith, because without faith and love we may destroy the world. With faith and love and no knowledge the world may also be destroyed.

I would propose that as each of us experiences and incorpo-rates the experiences of others, that we say among other pray-ers that we know we do not know. In the name of our belief that man is related to God through his fellowman, we humbly declare that we will seek the knowledge that will make it possible for us to become, in fact as well as in aspiration, our brothers' keepers.

VI Neighborhoods and Human Needs
(1966)

Human beings must be brought up among human beings who
have learned from other human beings how to live in a particular way. There are very few cultural differences when we discuss basic human needs; that is, the floor below which the
human being must not be permitted to fall.

Primarily, the neighborhood is the place where children are
brought up to become members of their own society. Inevitably, within a neighborhood children encounter various older
adults from whose experience they learn how to adapt themselves to the kind of society into which they are growing. In a
static society, older experienced people who have learned nothing new in their lifetime are the greatest asset, for they transmit
the entire heritage to the children. But in a society that is
changing, grandparents who are continually learning and who
have themselves participated in change have the highest potentiality for transmitting a sense of adaptation. The neighborhood,
where children learn to meet basic human needs and to move
toward the use of higher human capacities, is where they first
encounter adults—parents and grandparents and unrelated

adults of these two generations. The older people may not include their own grandparents (for in some parts of the world there is an extraordinary lack of tolerance of one's own relatives), but there will be some members of the grandparental generation who are treated with consideration.

Of course, any neighborhood that we design, or that we attempt to ameliorate, must meet the basic physiological needs for all human beings—the essential needs for food, water, space, sleep, rest, and a minimum of privacy.

Of these, privacy is one of the most variable. There are societies that have no word for privacy, and when the idea is explained to them they think it is horrible. In one society in which I worked—Samoa—a curtain hung between me and other members of the household gave me a certain privacy; but in a house without walls nothing separated me from the rest of the village, from whose eyes, obviously, I did not need the protection of privacy. Nevertheless, some sort of privacy, some small, identifiable spatial territory of one's own—even if it is only a hook on which to hang one's own hat—seems to be a basic human need.

A second basic need is for some continuity in human relationships. It need not be affectionate or even kind. One society that I studied—the Mundugumor—reared their children to be effective and happy cannibals, but Mundugumor methods of child rearing would seem very harsh to us. It never occurred to a mother to give her baby the breast when it cried; she would put it high on her shoulder to watch what was going on. A little baby was kept in a flat rough basket that was hung against the wall. When the baby became restless, she scratched the outside of the basket, making a sound like the squeak of chalk on a blackboard, and the baby stopped crying. It was not an affectionate sound, but it was a sound that assured the baby of continuity in its human evironment.

The idea that a baby must be brought up by its biological

mother and that it will be traumatized by the mother's absence for a week derives from a recognition of this need for continuity. But, in fact, the child who is reared from birth to be accustomed to eight different human beings, all of whom are close, can be given a sense of continuity by any one of them. And where the immediate environment—the shape of its bed and the smell of its room—is part of what is continuous, the child can stand a greater variety of persons close to it.

This means that in planning neighborhoods for the future, various possibilities are open to us. We can turn the family car into a house, and when the child, together with the cat and the dog and familiar toys, is moved to a strange place the car will still be a familiar home. Or we can bring children up to live in the same place every summer but in a different place each winter. We can do a great many different things, providing we keep in mind the basic need for continuity and familiarity. There is considerable evidence that failure to take this need into account may lead to severe conflict in young children, and so we are faced with the problem of how to move children safely from highly familiar to entirely unfamiliar environments, with nothing to bridge the gap. A familiar and trustworthy environment is necessary for the child to learn that things will be here tomorrow that are here today and that its hand, reaching out, will find what it is seeking for. But we must also recognize that continuity can be provided for in many different ways.

If children are to be ready to live in a changing world, they must also be prepared to deal with strangeness almost from the day of their birth. For those who live in the modern world it is a disabling experience to grow up knowing only their own relatives. The fewer the relatives, the more disabling an experience it is. And yet, all over the world, as older forms of the extended family are breaking down into small, isolated nuclear family groups, the child is becoming disastrously overdependent on its two parents. Disastrous in the sense that living in large

cities is disastrous for those who have not learned to deal with
a variety of people and who have not learned to expect that the
strange will be interesting and rewarding or to recognize that
it must be treated with a certain wariness.

The inclusion of the strange has implications for the size of
the basic neighborhood. That is, the neighborhood cannot be
modeled on the primitive village where everyone knows everyone else and everything is familiar. There are, however, some
people who would like to keep everything within a safe, closed
environment—keep all the cars out, keep all the strangers out,
and turn the neighborhood into a grass plot where all the children can run. There is no doubt that a neighborhood must have
something that is child-scale, some place where children can
walk about. I am inclined to think that if children can walk
enough, the question of whether or not adults are walkers is less
serious. Adults can tolerate enormous specialization—even
many kinds of deprivation—if, as children, their senses have
been stimulated. One striking example of this can be seen in the
experience of people who have suffered deafness, blindness, or
paralysis in later life, but who still can draw on earlier experience of hearing, vision, and movement. Helen Keller is probably the best example of such a person. She could hear and see
up to the time she learned her first word, and this early experience preserved for her a sense of the world that carried her
through her later incredible sensory isolation. All this suggests
that the better we can build into neighborhoods ways of human-
izing the small child in the fullest sense of the word, the greater
tolerance the adult will have for the strangeness and stresses of
a world in which some people may be physically highly restricted for long periods as they move into outer space or deep
in the sea—experiences for which human beings have had little
evolutionary preparation. Certainly, we need areas where
young children are safe and where they can move on their own
legs (and this, of course, will affect the location of nursery

schools and primary schools); but we also need to provide for their living dangerously part of the time, even while they are very young. Strangeness and danger are part of living in an urban environment.

The anonymity of the city is one of its strengths as well as—carried too far—one of its weaknesses. Even the young baby, growing up to live in a city, needs to have windows on the unknown world. The shopping center, in which the child encounters strangers and sees its mother encountering strangers, is one such window. But at the same time the child needs the grass plot, the protected walk, and the nursery school where everything is close and familiar. Only in this way can the small child achieve the autonomy that is necessary at every stage of development. There must be play places and front yards where children can walk safely without fear of traffic. When children move into a newly built housing estate that is inadequately protected from automobiles, parents may be so frightened that the children—who have no preparation for dealing with traffic—will run under the wheels of the cars, that they give the children no freedom of movement at all. In one tribe I know of, the village was located at some distance from a big river. Then one year the river changed its course and ran right through the village. The adults, who had no idea what to do, were terrified of the water and, of course, their children fell into the river. In contrast, another people who had lived on the river for a long time knew how to teach their children—and their children were safe. Today we have to teach our children not only about rivers, but also about traffic: to realize its dangers and be wary of them and also to know how to take chances safely. So, too, in every neighborhood there must be places where older children can move freely away from the familiar with confidence, trust, and toleration of strangers and the strange.

Children also need multisensory stimulation. There are several reasons for this. Because of tremendous individual differences, we do not know whether a particular child will be most dependent on hearing, sight, or touch. Moreover, in different contexts, there may be a greater emphasis on the use of the eyes or the use of the ears. The child who, as a small child, has lacked multisensory stimulation will be handicapped in making the necessary transition from one to the other. But, beyond these considerations, there is evidence that multisensory cross-referencing is a very creative source of innovation in thought, and we want to bring up children who have the capacity for innovation in a dynamic world.

Children need an environment in which they can learn fine discrimination—in which they can hear small sounds and learn to differentiate between footsteps, learn to hear slight differences in tones of voice, learn to wake and know what time it is. Some peoples have a greater sensitivity to noise and want to shut more of it out than other peoples do. This is something in which whole cultures can be differentiated one from another. But in all cultures, human beings—in order to be human—must understand the nonhuman. They must have some understanding of plants and animals, water and sunshine, earth, the stars, the moon and the sun. People who have not appreciated the stars cannot really appreciate satellites; they are confused as to which is which. This need to know about the nonhuman also affects what is necessary for a good neighborhood. There must be water, preferably water that moves, for moving water is one of the major experiences through which a child's senses are amplified. There must also be earth—not merely a sandbox. There must be animals, although not necessarily large animals. A child can learn about animals as well from fish in a pond as from buffalo on a prairie, and he can dig in a miniature garden as well as in a great field.

Providing the pattern is complete, the scale can be reduced and the details of the arrangement can be different in different neighborhoods. The child needs to learn what lives in the water, what lives in the air, what lives on the earth, and how human beings are related to these growing, living, singing, fighting, and playing creatures. Any environment is crippling if it cuts the child off from such experiences. The child who has grown up in peach country—who has learned to register, as he wakes up, a drop in temperature and knows how this will affect what people do—has acquired a lifetime familiarity. He can live in a city for forty years, but when he goes back to the peach country and sees the peach blossoms, he can still wake up at two o'clock in the morning and say what the people are going to do. Experience of this kind is never lost.

A principal aim in building a neighborhood must be to give the child trust, confidence, and the kind of autonomy that can be translated into a strength to bear the strange, the unknown, and the peculiar. So children need some experience of the range of humanity in its different versions. It is nonsense that children do not have racial prejudices. Of course, they do not know which race is "superior," and this is the root of racial prejudice. However, children are sensitive to differences in physique, and a child to whom only dark-skinned people are familiar may get used to seeing white faces but shriek with terror at the sight of a white man in a bathing suit. Equally well, a white child may get used to seeing dark faces but be terrified at the discovery that the middle of someone's back is dark. We need an environment in which the child experiences differences in color, type, and physique with sufficient range so that no one group is solely associated with unskilled labor or with the exercise of some highly skilled profession. Instead of being presented with stereotypes by age, sex, color, class, or religion, children must have the opportunity to learn that within each range, some people are loathsome and some are delightful.

I think we must consider how children can be presented with models of the kinds of thinking that will be required of most educated adults. Though not all children will learn in the same way, in general it is known, for example, that children who have grown up in rooms that conform to ordinary geometric forms later learn geometric thinking with relative ease. Similarly, children can learn about volumes and ratios from blocks long before they learn words to express the ideas they have grasped. And today they need somehow to learn that their own language is only one of many languages. They need to experience the fact that this object—this container for holding liquids—is called "glass" *in English*. This is something that must be learned very early, but it is part of learning that one's own culture is one of many cultures. It is part of acquiring freedom of movement in the modern world.

In building a neighborhood that meets human needs we start with the needs of infants. These give us the groundwork on which we can build for contact with other human beings, with the physical environment, with the living world, and with the experiences through which the individual's full humanity can be realized. For every culture the criteria must be modified. We cannot set our sights too low, but we can aim at any height, for we have as yet scarcely begun to explore human potentialities. How these are developed will depend on the learning experiences we can provide for children through the human habitat in which they live. This is our moral, even religious, obligation to each other.

VII   Spiritual Issues
in the Problem of Birth Control
(1953)

The problem of birth control has been called "the great religious issue of the modern world." This judgment can be made whether one speaks very broadly about the question of how the underdeveloped countries of the world are to share in the technical benefits which the overdeveloped, less highly reproductive countries have attained; speaks more narrowly in terms of the conflicts between rising nationalisms with their recurrent tendency to emphasize the production of more and more cannon fodder; or more narrowly still, of the issue between Catholicism and secular and Protestant proponents of planned parenthood in regard to birth-control and abortion legislation. This is a question which is pointed up sharply by the condition which prevailed in France where contraceptives and contraceptive information were legislated against, and abortion reached the appalling ratio of an estimated one abortion to one live birth. If we turn from these very large-scale conflicts to the spiritual front on which modern man is attempting, under God, to adapt the tenets of earlier ages to the exigencies of the modern world, the issue remains a significant one.

On the side of human dignity it is argued (and cogently) that to reach full spiritual stature man—and woman—must be free to choose between one course of action and another, and that contraception gives women control over their own fertility, a freedom denied them when a wedded wife was held to owe conjugal duties to her husband, whatever the outcome in long series of unwanted pregnancies—many of them bound to end in miscarriage—still births, and early infant deaths. On the side of public health it is argued that only by reducing the infant death rate and simultaneously lowering the infant birth rate is it possible to give the underfed peoples of the world, whose lives are now made a burden by poverty, hunger, and disease, that measure of economic dignity which, once glimpsed as a possibility, cannot be denied to any people without a regression in man's responsibility for other men.

There are additional smaller issues. The birth-control issue has been chosen in certain countries as a battleground between organized Catholic and Protestant forces or, more significantly perhaps, between organized Catholic groups and organized lay groups, with the Protestant and Jewish religious groups playing an indeterminate and mixed role. Under these circumstances the whole matter becomes a blur in which the Catholic participants in any discussion often carry the whole burden of defending not only their own particular religious position but *all* religious positions against a secular statement, supported by the participation of liberal Jews, often with no representative of organized Protestant religious life—on the convenient theory that anyone who is not labeled as Jewish or Catholic is *ipso facto* some kind of Protestant. There are small intensive controversies based on studies of child psychology, in which the proponents of one side cite the better adjustment of children who are born very close together, while the others argue for spaced births, or for the superiority in character of children who come from enormous happy families where they were reared in a sort of superior junior republic with enough brothers and sisters to form a basketball team—undoubtedly a halcyon condition for any child—as compared with the adjustment of children whose parents never achieved such a full and teeming nursery.

Or the battleground may shift to such ambitious theories as those advanced by David Riesman in *The Lonely Crowd**—that there is an identifiable difference in the character of men reared in a society with a growing population, and that from such a society we may expect the inner-directed man—a technical phrase for the man of conscience who holds firmly by the precepts of his upbringing and is capable of applying them perseveringly within changing circumstances. The same type of thesis was suggested by Robert Lamb in his work on Fall River —that a growing community has a kind of moral zest and purpose which is lacking in one that is declining in population, although here the emphasis was more on symptoms of integration in better social services than in its expression in individual character. The shift from the use of man's efforts from production to consumption, within an economy which is conceived as mature and closed, characterized by Riesman's "other-directed man" has been prettily summed up in the witticism that families that are going up in the world live in large houses with attics, while families that have "arrived" live in small houses with rumpus rooms in the basement.

Primitive societies also provide us with vivid demonstrations of how a general spiritual malaise resulting from a destructive clash between old values and those of the more complex cultures with which they come in contact may be accompanied by a falling birthrate and a form of race suicide unassisted by any change in practices of birth control or infanticide. It seems that,

*Rev. ed. 1964.

like children reared in institutions without personalized care, the children of a people who have lost their sense of the meaning of life may themselves also die, wasting away from lack of a will to live.

All of these questions are becoming more acute at the present time, for the borders of our political and social and religious consciousness are widening around us and our thinking must encompass the whole of mankind—as actual Burmese or Akikiyu or Canadians or Argentinians or Frenchmen, not merely in the abstract form of the brotherhood of man. They are perhaps easier to face today in a period of an upsurge in the birth rate based not upon any nationalistic push for population or any new restriction upon birth control, but rather upon the desire of young Americans to have several children. The timidity of the prosperous twenties when parents calculating ahead to the cost of teeth straightening and a college education felt they could only "afford" two children—a decision comparable to the self-imposed limitation of families in France—has given place to a willingness to have several children, which the grandparents, often called upon to help support them, feel as a strange comment on their own caution and self-denial. In the United States children are becoming an experience to be sought in its own right, not only out of duty to God or to State, to the inheritance or the preponderance of one ethnic group over another, not to farm or manage the mill or carry on the secrets of a craft, but because the experience of bringing human beings into the world and participating in the early years of their growth is a rewarding one for men and women alike. The strength of this present tendency can be measured in the low interest women take in careers as such and the time young fathers spend with their children.

Here in the United States, we are in a period of high prosperity with the highest standard of living mankind has ever know, unpressed by nationalist urgings to increase our population—as happens in totalitarian states. We are unfrightened by a fear of falling behind in a competitive population race—as was France vis-à-vis Germany between the two Wars, or French Canadians versus English Canadians. We are unterrified by the disproportion between a changing survival rate and our natural resources which becomes obvious in any Eastern country when public health measures are first introduced. We live within a tradition of freedom of State from Church which underwrites our rejection of the control of legislation by any religious group. We are in a period when young people want children. So it is here in the United States that we can face squarely some of the spiritual issues involved. In all probability we will see in the next few years a method of oral contraception (contraceptive drugs taken by mouth) developed which will sweep away the variety of problems of cost, education, and side effect on the nervous organization of practitioners of contraception and leave us with a clear central issue: what to do about contraception in marriage. (Extramarital use of contraception will undoubtedly take care of itself, especially if religious groups maintain their present attitudes about sex.)

Here I want to focus on one very simple point: what one tells one's child about the choices which lie back of its existence. "Why was I born, Mother?" "Why did you have me?" "Why did you have another baby when we were so poor?" "Why did you and Mother keep on having girls, Daddy, until you got to me? Are boys better than girls?" Within the climate of opinion of modern America, with its emphasis on choice and freedom of action, there seems to be a clear alternative. If we are able to answer, as can the Catholic who fulfills in act as well as in faith the dictates of the Church, "When your father and I married, that was our welcome to you as one of the children whom God sent us. Poor or rich, sick or well, we make a home for those whom God sends us. Bright or stupid, physically perfect or physically handicapped, the children that God sends us are ours. It is our task [as the Order devoted to the care of severely handicapped children puts it] to help each child make a contribution in time as well as in Eternity." This is one answer, an answer which affords full dignity to the parents obeying the will of God and to the children whom God has sent.

If, on the other hand, one does not agree that sex without the willingness to welcome the children who result from it is spiritually wrong, but feels instead that sex is a form of expression between those who love each other and share each other's lives, and that children should be planned for, each child's arrival specifically heralded, not by an angel's song, but by parental choice—then the answer to the child's questions seems just as surely prescribed. For then, ideally, one must be able to say, "We wanted another child. We knew that it might be a boy or a girl and that which sex you were was outside our power of control. We knew that *whether* we had a child or not when we were ready to have one was also outside our control. But all we could do to make ready for you we did. We chose to have a child, and you were born within that choice." But the in-between position, the position of those whose children are phrased as various degrees of unfortunate accidents—a phrasing which is open also to Catholics who may say to their children that they prayed the Lord wouldn't send them one more mouth to feed—seems a profoundly unspiritual one. "We wanted children sometimes, of course, but not just yet, but something went wrong with our birth control." "We had two children and that was enough—I thought we were safely beyond the danger of having another." However much most parents who speak—or act—in terms of partial, faulty, poorly persisted-in contraception, or equally partial, poorly persisted-in traditional Catholic doctrine that the only acceptable way of refusing the gift of children is by total abstention from sex relations—or in countries where the "Rhythm" has been found acceptable, abstention during a period of possible fertility—

may, once the child is on its way, welcome it and love it, it is a damaging thing to do to a child to phrase its birth as an accident, something for which its parents did not properly prepare, something which they would not have chosen.

Much of our philosophy of child rearing in this country is based upon a sense of the poignancy of the child's possible cry: "I did not ask to be born." But an increasing awareness of the dignity of the child as a full person forces us to recognize the equally poignant cry: "You didn't want me to be born." Between complete acceptance of a religious dicta that one may not create the conditions within which a child may be conceived without being willing to welcome its advent, and complete care to use contraceptives with a responsible insistence that there will be no "accidents," there lies a middle ground which presents a grave spiritual challenge to the modern world.

It may be that we are able to face this issue more clearly because of the position of women today, both as educated mothers able to understand the findings of modern dynamic psychology, and as practitioners in these modern fields of research and application—child development, child psychiatry, anthropology, social work. Women's relationship to pregnancy and birth lacks the historical ambiguity which has surrounded the father's role; the moral position of the individual who must face directly the physical consequences of any act is clearer, less equivocal, than that of one who must deal with the results of a mutual act which are then lived out within the body of another person. In any event the fully human realization and solution of any problem requires the contribution of both sexes, each acting in educational competence and spiritual responsibility.

VIII The Liberal Church in an Urban Community
(1964)

Before discussing the challenges presented to the liberal church by the urban community, it might be best to specify my use of the word "liberal." While this phrase is often used to denote a church which is liberal in doctrine, my designation will be a church which is liberal in relation to society. The liberal believes that social change can and should be beneficial. Contrasted with this is the conservative position that what the world needs are not new social forms, but stricter application of the old forms. I believe that to stay alive, society must have both liberals, who wish to work responsibly for new forms, and conservatives, who wish to work responsibly for the old ones. A society in which everyone takes either the liberal or the conservative position would be essentially lacking in dynamic tension.

When a church defines itself as liberal—in this wider sense—it immediately establishes a special relationship with society. The liberal church encourages in its membership a responsible interest in social change—on this earth, now; it becomes, inevitably, somewhat involved in politics; it can no longer interest all the members of the community in which it is situated. Within our contemporary society a church which takes an outspokenly liberal or outspokenly conservative position attracts those who, to some degree, have an informed knowledge of conditions and who wish a discussion of those conditions to be part of the substance of sermons, talks, or study groups. This further limits the potential congregation to those who are interested in combining religious membership with the use of their minds on essentially temporal questions. Such a church requires from the clergy a type of educational background and contemporary interest in public matters that is not required in a church which takes no official position on social issues. Since both the clergy and laymen in a liberal church may also be expected to be more intellectual, those who have neither the education nor the interest to participate in discussions on current affairs are not attracted to such a church program.

So I believe that we can speak as if the effective membership of the liberal church comes from those whose intellectual commitment to social change is combined with some genuine religious motivation. Therefore, no matter whether the congregation feel that they are free from intellectual snobbery or social snobbery of any sort, such a congregation will consist of largely one kind of people, drawn from the religious segment of the liberal segment of the intellectually minded of the educated section of our society. There may be some attempt to compensate for the narrow limits of inclusion by emphasizing the presence of members of minority groups—with the same educational qualifications—the greater possibilities of participation offered women, youth, or foreigners. Superficially, this will appear to compensate for the high degree of selectivity, but the selectivity will remain. "Wherever you find Unitarians, you find intelligent, educated people" is one of the clichés which describes such a situation.

The limiting feature of its self-definition presents a problem for the liberal church as a whole. Any institution or organization in contemporary American culture which is exclusive in any way becomes a target for criticism for reasons with which the contemporary liberal must agree, at least in principle. In the current battle for racial integration the rights of most groups to organize along the lines of similarity of background or commonality of interest are under attack. The institution which by its nature and definition excludes large sections of the human race must try to atone for this in various explicit ways. If the American Association of University Women is, as it must, to refuse graduates of unrecognized colleges, then it must be more careful about its treatment of all the graduates at recognized colleges—whatever their race, religion, or class—than a less exclusive organization need be. In fact, the League of Women Voters does technically admit men. Men's clubs are being deserted in favor of clubs which admit women and children. This persistent, unremitting pressure for egalitarian nonexclusiveness places the liberal church, with its selectivity along intellectual lines, in a very exposed position.

Much of this pressure for nonexclusiveness comes from an attitude which disguises a deep envy of the more fortunate by using phrases like fair play or a sense of justice. In a great majority of cases these phrases do not indicate a generous desire to include, protect, and cherish the less privileged, but rather a desperate determination to prevent the existence of more privileged people. I saw a vivid example of this attitude some time ago, when I proposed, as a moral exercise, that the question of air raid shelters be discussed, not in the context of American survival alone, but for the entire human race. To do this I proposed that a representative group from the recently married, young, still childless population of every nation be resident always—in successive groups—in blast-proof shelters. Although I stressed that this choice would indeed be a cross section of socioeconomic statuses, races, intelligence, and creeds, the suggestion elicited just two responses, in public or private, from Americans. The liberals—who had made the word shelter into a magical invocation of evil—denounced the suggestion. The nonliberals discussed just one point: It would be unfair to save one group. They went further and transmuted what I had said into a program for saving an elite group—it was turned into a eugenicist program. They were really asking only one question: "Is somebody else going to have a better chance to be saved than I myself, or my children? If so, it's wrong and I'm against it."

At the risk of incurring the anger of the liberals I take the position that emphasis on equalization of opportunity, which is simply designed to decrease privilege, is essentially self-defeating, and stifles possibilities for the more privileged to participate responsibly in the lives of the less privileged.

The difference between the egalitarianism which simply attacks privilege and the position which maintains some possibility of greater responsibility is well illustrated by the tax exemption provisions of contemporary American and British income tax laws. The American laws make it easy for the rich to give, at a ridiculously small percentage on the dollar, to educational and charitable causes. The British law not only takes a higher percentage of personal income from the wealthy, but watches more jealously over any alleged exemption for good works, requiring a much more cumbersome long-term program of the would-be giver. One desirable reform in the United States would be to make it easier for those with small incomes to engage in voluntary giving.

But our educational system has responded to the demand for more education for the children of the uneducated by lowering educational standards. The Soviet Union, with an egalitarian ethic which demanded the privileges of the aristocracy for the peasant and the worker, insisted that the children of the uneducated be given the old type of education—that which was once reserved for the children of the highly privileged. In the United States solution to this problem everyone loses, because everyone who gets a secondary school education gets a poorer one, whereas in the Soviet Union everyone gains. Egalitarianism which is negative simply destroys a resource. Under compulsion from this kind of egalitarianism, the responsibility of the more privileged for the less privileged becomes transformed into an impersonal—and consequently less demanding—type of social responsibility for community chests, hospital boards, housing reforms, and social legislation.

Members of a liberal religious body find it difficult to satisfy their feelings of social responsibility by impersonal forms of participation which obscure class or ethnic differences. One of the essential messages of Christianity is that of the brotherhood of man, exemplified when Jesus washed the feet of his disciples. Under the inspiration of the Christian ethic noble ladies and respectable women nursed the poor and the dissolute. One appeal of Christian missions has always been its inclusiveness. Where Christianity's inclusiveness has been compromised by considerations of race or class or nationality, less exclusive religions have obtained the people's allegiance instead. Within our own nation, and more conspicuously in such places as the Caribbean countries, the small sects which appeal directly to the poor and the uneducated and give them a role in the management of their churches are growing much more rapidly than the older Christian churches which have a more stratified dependence on the role of the privileged in the conduct of church affairs.

The liberal church may argue that some people simply stay away from a church which excludes no one and the church is therefore not responsible for an appearance of exclusiveness. An overdressed congregation sitting in overstuffed pews may also argue that no one is kept out—those who stay away do so because they just don't feel comfortable. Such an overdressed congregation can dress simply and make the poor welcome. But a liberal church, relying as it does on education and intellectualism, will find it more difficult to make the uneducated welcome. The membership cannot simply discard its education, its vocabulary, its dependence on the written word, and a literate knowledge of contemporary affairs. Much more than a few acts of simple friendliness would be required for the typical congregation of a liberal church to make those unlike themselves really welcome.

At present this situation does not concern the suburban liberal church deeply. In a one-class suburb the liberal church can absorb the liberals, leaving the conservatives and indifferents of the same class and ethnic group to join the other churches and synagogues. The demand that religious organizations also provide for the social life of adolescents and adults can be met comfortably. No one is left out; the addition of social activities —scouts, dances, church suppers—merely ensures that one's children meet—and hopefully marry—the "right kind" of young people. Exclusiveness without hierarchy—which is substantially the condition in the new suburbs—presents little immediate challenge to one's religious conscience. The choice of separation from one's fellowman was made at quite a safe distance from one's present life when one chose that particular suburb. From then on the liberal young people of the community can study about ethnic minorities, integration, underdeveloped countries, about starvation and deprivation and what should be done about them—without any pressure for a greater degree of egalitarianism for Christian charity in the present. They can contribute money to good causes, and perhaps someday join the Peace Corps or the National Service Corps.

In such suburban areas where the self-selection of the educated and the concerned does not press too heavily on their conscience, they can argue, and I believe with real cogency, that they are gathered together to increase their special kind of ability to be of service to the world. They can argue that they want to think about man's needs and that while it is possible to pray together with every other member of the human race, it is considerably less possible to talk together coherently.

It is possible for a dedicated minority to withdraw from the world and yet devote all their hearts and all their souls and all their minds to finding a way to make life better for their fellowmen. They may see prayer as the way and live a cloistered life; they may seek to compensate for great exclusiveness by increased social responsibility as the Society of Friends has done; they may live in hotel rooms in Washington, work for a national organization, and see practically nothing of their fellowmen. They may hold retreats among green fields, establish schools and colleges where their children can learn harmony with nature.

But there seem to be some inherent requirements about the kind of barriers which are drawn in face-to-face situations which we disregard at great spiritual risk. "Long contact with those whose lot we are powerless to ameliorate breeds a subtle contempt." The day-by-day passing by on the other side—however little those whom one passes wish to partake of a fellowship which it would be quite hopeless to offer—involves a daily look of indifference and inattention that becomes frozen on the human face.

If there is a dramatic contrast between the liberal churchgoer's estate and that of those who live just outside the church door, this uncomfortable distance is inescapable. Urban renewal is going forward, conditions in the new projects are very bad, juvenile crime is increasing, drug addiction is increasing, young vandals threaten the church so that it has to be kept tightly locked and is no longer open to the passing stranger. If there are evening church activities, the neighborhood may be too dangerous for members to go home alone at night. A next step might be calling police to protect them until they get out of the neighborhood. Such situations are, I believe, ethically unmanageable and lead, in many if not all cases, to solutions which are spiritually debilitating. Often the solutions consist of diluted settlement-house type of activites for the under-privileged. The church is rented for graduation ceremonies for minority groups from poor schools; it may run a child guidance clinic or a nursery school for working mothers; it may offer its parking lot for neighborhood children to play in. But unless the members of the church—especially the young people—can actually participate in some of these activities, the line between those on whose behalf one labors—but with whom one has no activities in common—and oneself, becomes unbearable.

Thus the liberal urban church faces a more difficult situation than does the liberal suburban church. A church which appeals to the well educated automatically finds itself in special circumstances in the city, where a few blocks away the deprived, the desperately poor, the dispossessed live. No amount of nominal hospitality—invitations to which there will be no acceptance—is going to blind the eyes of the liberal congregation to the juveniles loitering on corners, to the derelict lying drunk in the gutter, to the poorly cared for, anxious children. The urban church cannot comfortably avoid a very serious reconsideration of its position if it tries to maintain its aloofness and yet claims to be committed to the interest of the great masses of dispossessed people who more and more are constituting our urban populations.

The problem is additionally hard for those churches which depend very heavily on the leadership provided by the minister. Such churches are far less interchangeable than are churches which rely on liturgy and worship. Churches of the latter type, when the neighborhood changes and members of the old congregation move away, will find many members among the new population. City-wide organizations can take over some costs if the new congregation is too poor to carry them; the building remains in use, related to the neighborhood. Coping with population shifts is more difficult for the urban Unitarian church with its more intellectually aware congregation, dependent upon a special type of intellectual leadership. Such a church cannot easily substitute one congregation for another. It must seek somehow to continue to attract its former congregation or new members of the same kind as the former members—in neither case will it recruit the poor uneducated who live in such appallingly large numbers close by.

The situation is little better when the liberal Church stands in a neighborhood which is now a downtown business district, the streets crowded from Monday to Friday, hushed and silent over the weekend. Here the question is not the haunting awareness of the deprived outside the door. Rather the problem is a fragmentation of life that is represented when the working population unites to use the downtown church for weekday study groups and scatters to worship in many different suburban churches on weekends. The church whose congregation is united by liturgy and worship rather than by commonality of interest here, again, has an advantage. The Roman Catholic can attend a mass on a holy day of obligation, in any church, near work or near his residence, on a trip, without any sense of fragmentation at all. The church is one, while men's residences and places of work are many. But the Unitarian church is not so homogeneous; it depends upon each individual minister to weld his congregation into a unit, in which a common responsible and intellectual approach to life is vivid and significant. The use of the downtown church for weekday study groups and services therefore presents different problems. Unless the downtown church is somehow tied in with the group of suburban churches where people give their weekend allegiances, participation in two churches is not likely to work.

A step toward solving the peculiar situation of the "weekday" liberal church would be for churches to arrange a planned interaction between the two areas of work and residence. In many ways the liberal church may find it easier to interest people from the working world around it than from the self-conscious new suburbs. The suburban church could continue to perform its extracurricular purposes of social segmentation and matchmaking among housewives, children, and youth; the urban church in a business district could then be directed toward adults—a locally working population on weekdays, and a totally different congregation, city-wide, nationwide, international, on Sundays, a population which was transient but oriented to the same values. In this way visitors to the city who cared about the liberal religious tradition would always have a place to go.

The urban church has opportunity at its doorstep. If it is located in a business district, it might do much more to provide ongoing religious resources for the working population. Churches which exist solely as a place for people to pray and receive the sacraments can exist anywhere. What the liberal church offers most conspicuously are chances to listen, discuss, think about, read, and discuss again such topics as technological change or the century of the common man. This desire for active interrelationship with the like-minded is present in many people who spend their working days in business areas and who do not necessarily find the Sunday morning service in their one-class suburb as stimulating as it might be. The downtown church that is always open at noon, and for two hours after work hours, that provides opportunities to eat cheaply and talk enormously, that has a library on relevant subjects, shows films on what is going on in other parts of the world—that is frankly oriented to a population who only work near the church—could go a long way.

Finally, there is the case of the urban liberal church located in a residential district of poor housing and poor social conditions. If it can be set up to provide avenues of development for those in the community, then its location can remain not only tolerable, but it will be in a position to provide its members with opportunities of personal action—called by the more orthodox by the old-fashioned word "witness"—which will make their church membership more real to them.

To meet this challenge the members must have a great deal of time to spare, to go out and work among those to whom they have nothing to offer inside the church. They must develop ways of picking up very rapidly the few eager, aspiring youngsters who are attracted to a wider type of education and responsibility. The old institution of the settlement—almost abandoned in this period of organized charity and aggressive egalitarianism—was based on a very sound principle. To help those young people in a slum neighborhood who wished to learn how to escape from the limitations of their environment, the helpers had to live among them. The young people needed more than a club leader on Thursday afternoons; they needed to know what the room looked like in which someone who reads books—for delight—lived. They still need this. The urban liberal church can become such a center, if there is a place where the minister and a group of interested people, young and old, will really live and work out into the neighborhood—in human terms.

The principal tie between the young people of the deprived group and the young people of the privileged room will be aspiration—a human tie based upon an intellectual aspiration for social mobility. Unfortunately, such upward mobility has been described by a limited and noncomparative social science as status-striving; a cold innuendo which may hamper the church member's attempts at understanding in what ways it is worthy of respect. Or he may be hampered by a certain amount of sentimentality about the greater honesty and sincerity of the dispossessed. (A few months of close contact should disabuse his mind of any sentimental notion that poverty breeds goodness.)

Once any group in society stands in a relatively deprived position in relation to other groups, it is genuinely deprived. The Eskimo living among his snows had very little of what we would call wealth—but he was not poor—and he could be proud. The poverty of our industrial society is of quite a different order—something to be fought about and done away with. Meanwhile, because it has been widely recognized that far-reaching social changes are necessary to establish a point below which we cannot afford ethically to let anyone sink, there has been a corresponding devaluation of individual "good works," of the person who spends time in attempting to improve the lot of a particular child or adolescent, to denigrate mere personal good works as belonging to the old category of "Lady Bountiful." But it was from the concern of the highly motivated Lady Bountifuls—the Roman widows who turned their homes into the first hospitals for the poor, the Florence Nightingales and the Jane Addamses, that the awakened social conscience and social legislation sprang.

Within the liberal church membership it is not so much money as other sorts of bounty which are available for sharing. In every slum area, with crowded schools, harassed teachers, and inadequate resources, there are young people who are hungering and thirsting after knowledge, after the intellectual, the artistic, the scientific life. They go into our public libraries and take down the books. They pick out Keats or Gerard Manley Hopkins—with a sure inner ear they know these books are their birthright. They get a college chemistry book and pore over it —but there is no place in their crowded homes to try an experiment. No one buys them a chemistry set. The school laboratory —often raided by gangs bent only on destruction—is locked up after school hours.

There is no road out for them unless it is provided by individuals. The only way to find out what books really mean is to know people who read. The only way to understand how religious dedication and a burning desire for a better life for human beings can be responsibly related—through increased knowledge of the way the world is organized—is to know people who are deeply committed to doing just that. Face-to-face contact becomes more, not less, valuable as the world becomes more complex.

The liberal church has at least these choices before it: isolation in a one-class neighborhood; concentration on the working rather than the residential life; participation, person-to-person, face-to-face, in the life of the deprived if the church is situated in such a neighborhood.

Within the historic Christian church different vocations and different purposes were served by the establishment of religious orders; each order could follow its own rule, selectively and exclusively. One order could concentrate on study, another on prayer, another on good works done with human hands on behalf of other human beings. Within our modern fragmented world these complementary but not mutually exclusive activities have to be carried out by denominations which are separated one from another by dogma and difference in practice, and, often enough, difference in socioeconomic status. To the extent that the congregation of a church seeks to become a religious community, there is a demand that the church develop and serve the whole man, and all men. Any rationale for concentrating on one kind of service, or one kind of parishioner, will inevitably conflict with this demand. Only a Christian community which had a place for every style of worship and many variants of revelation would make a division of labor between Unitarian and Universalist, Methodist, Presbyterian, Friends, Jehovah's Witnesses, Roman Catholics and the Greek Orthodox completely spiritually tolerable. In the meantime, all solutions are a kind of mend and make do—necessary so that a generation does not grow up with its spiritual life cut off at the roots.

IX A Religious System
with Science at Its Core
(1970)

While scientists are describing the dire effects of an imbalance
in nature as a result of the technological advances and population explosion of the last fifty years, and while politicians are
trying to formulate workable programs for bringing these ex-
cesses of modern society under control, our young people are
looking for models of some different relationship, some different way of thinking of man-in-nature instead of—in a metaphor
from a recent presidential address—the war between man and
nature. The young have turned to Asian religions in which
doctrines of reincarnation have elevated the position of all living things, however minute, to possible embodiment of past or
future human souls; to Africa, where the fertility of the land and
the fertility of living things are bound together by ties to the
ancestors; and to the American Indians, whose early prophets
were horrified at the European agriculture that cut off the hair
of Mother Earth or drove deep into her breast.

In this turn away-or-back for models we can recognize two
potentialities: (1) the development of an eclectic worldwide
ethic of conservation that will include not only the Judeo-Chris-

tian ideas of man given dominion over nature, of man as cus-
todian of God's world and thus taking a latter-day part in creation, but also the ideas of the other continents, the outcome of
which might be among other things vegetarianism; or (2) an
entirely new synthesis between religion and science.

Such a synthesis would take into account all of our new, intricate knowledge of the web of life. It would distinguish between
the kind of applications of science modeled on physics and
chemistry—where there is an attempt to maximize one factor
at the expense of another—and those applications based on
biology, where optimization rather than maximization is
sought. It would use the recognition that when man permitted
himself to become alienated from part of himself, elevating
rationality and often narrow purpose above those ancient intuitive properties of the mind that bind him to his biological past,
he was in effect cutting himself off from the rest of the natural
world. It would use also the recognition that among human
beings, individuality has reached such a high point that each of
us, as he or she matures, becomes a special version of the entire
environment, almost a separate species in himself or herself.

Recognizing man's place in the natural world would make a
change in much of our thinking about society. In the past we
have thought about individuals as grouped together in families,
families in clans, clans in tribes or villages, and villages, towns,
and finally cities bound together in nations. It may well be that
we should be thinking instead of each individual or group as
part of a sector of the total environment, with the air he
breathes and the earth upon which he walks as a unit that has
to be taken into account. Nationhood, replacing nationalism,
would include the total environment: earth below, sky above,
lakes and rivers and edges of the sea, not as territory but as part
of being. Our increasing recognition of earth as a planet seen
from the moon, an island limited in natural resources and need-

ing to husband them, is bound to contribute to such a new point of view.

There are many harbingers of the new ways of thinking. Vegetarianism is now a sufficient badge of new attitudes that those who live nearby a group of idealistic young vegetarians may be called "meat eaters." Special attention, care, and reverence are accorded those species of bird or fish that are in danger of extinction, and the bald eagle can become an object of protective care rather than an incitement to patriotic partisanship. The use of American Indian costume is another way in which some of the young especially interested in symbolism are reidentifying with the land where the Indian dwelt so long in a simple and symbiotic relationship, where a fisherman returned the bones of his catch to the stream so that it might be born again, to serve once more as food for man.

The relationship of primitive man to his environment can, however, be very much overromanticized. Indians who had lived for centuries in a comfortable relationship to game without exterminating it, rapidly slaughtered the buffalo when given firearms. Faced with new and much more destructive hunting weapons, they showed no more restraint than modern man has shown in his headlong manufacturing of nondegradable plastics or insoluble detergents. The Australian aborigine, who had developed a nomadic life precisely related to the sanitation demands of the desert, carried little of his careful habits over when he camped near a modern town. The very delicacy of the earlier adjustment of the Asian peasant who recycled human waste, of the Eskimo tabooing seafood when land food was available, only point up the way each age must make its own style of relating to the environment.

The contemporary demand for immediacy (for art that is created now and for the moment only) may well be given a technological expression and deal with one aspect of our destruction of the environment: we might perhaps demand that everything we use has a short and predetermined life-span, that beer cans and soft-drink bottles be so constituted of completely degradable elements that once used, they return to be "brother to the insensible rock and to the sluggish clod." Our clothes might also be made of materials that, when they disintegrate, as they already do, are returned to become a resource for future clothes. Instead of a world weighed down and cluttered with outmoded things, we could combine the need for new work—through which our vast populations could be paid and thus fed —with the need to conserve what we have and to keep the world free of waste.

Earlier models can also serve a purpose. So some African conservationists permit hunting, but only with a bow and arrow, weapons that once left man and game in a fair balance.

But it is good to recognize that ever since man discovered how to make fire, he has been changing the face of the earth, sometimes controlling it in extortionist and exploitive activities or by religious exercises and taboos. But he has never before been faced with what he is capable of today: the power to destroy every living thing on this planet at least five times over (the unreality of this whole situation is reflected in the term "overkill"), and the power to make the planet uninhabitable within a matter of a few decades.

The original tale of Adam and Eve who ate of the tree of knowledge of good and evil pales before the lost innocence of men who can now destroy not only the little patch of woodland that they call their own and not only many other men, but the whole earth and all men. For such a loss of innocence and such a new responsibility we have no models either among primitive men or the ancient religions. We will have to move instead in the direction suggested by Buckminster Fuller: toward man's responsibility to the fact that he represents the highest capacity to introduce order in the known universe. We need a religious system with science at its very core, in which the traditional opposition between science and religion, reflected in grisly truth by our technologically desecrated countryside, can again be resolved, but in terms of the future instead of the past.

X The Future As the Basis for Establishing a Shared Culture (1965)

The Present Situation

The world today is struggling with many kinds of disjuncture. Some derive from the progressive fragmentation of what was once a whole—as higher education has broken down into a mass of separate specialties. Some have come about with the development of world views that parallel and often contradict older and displaced—but not replaced—ways of viewing the world. Others result from a juxtaposition of vastly different and extremely incongruent world views within the national and also the worldwide context provided by our contemporary press and television coverage. Within the framework of the United Nations we have balloting for representatives both from countries with many hundreds of years of high civilization and from countries just emerging from a primitive way of life. Still others are the effect of changing rates in the production of knowledge, which bring about unexpected discrepancies between the young and the old. In a sense these different kinds of disjuncture can also be seen as related to the very diverse ways in which the emergent, changing world is experienced by people of different ages—particularly young children—who are differently placed in the world, the nation, and the community.

Discussion of this tremendous fragmentation and of the agglomerations of partly dissociated, historically divergent, and conceptually incongruent patterns has been conducted, too often, in a narrow or a piecemeal fashion which takes into account only certain problems as they affect certain groups. The "two cultures" discussion is an example of such an approach, in which neither the arts nor the social sciences are included in what is essentially a lament about the state of communication within a small sector of the English-speaking world, whose members for various reasons of contemporary position or achievement think of themselves as an elite. In another context it is demanded that children's textbooks should portray "realistically" the conditions in which many American children live, because the conventional house pictured in advertisements and schoolbooks is unreal to the underprivileged children who live in cabins and coldwater flats and tenements. Even though the aim was to rectify the consequences of social and economic fragmentation at one level, a literal response to this demand would result in further fragmentation of our culture at another level. Wherever we turn, we find piecemeal statements, each of which can be regarded as a separate and partial definition of the basic problem of disjuncture, and piecemeal attempts at solution, each of which, because of the narrowness of the context in which it is made, produces new and still more complicated difficulties.

Yet these partial definitions and attempts at solution point in the same direction. We are becoming acutely aware that we need to build a culture within which there is better communication—a culture within which interrelated ideas and assumptions are sufficiently widely shared so that specialists can talk with specialists in other fields, specialists can talk with laymen,

laymen can ask questions of specialists, and the least educated can participate, at the level of political choice, in decisions made necessary by scientific or philosophical processes which are new, complex, and abstruse.

Models for intercommunication of this kind—poorly documented but made vividly real through the treatment given them by historians—already exist, in the past, within our own tradition. One model, of which various uses have been made, is the Greek city, where the most erudite man and the simplest man could enjoy the same performance of a tragedy. Another, in which there has been a recent upsurge of interest, is medieval Europe, where the thinker and the knight, the churchman, the craftsman, and the serf could read a view of the world from the mosaic on the wall, the painting above the altar, or the carving in the portico, and all of them, however far apart their stations in life, could communicate within one framework of meaning. But such models are not limited to the distant past. Even much more recently, in Victorian England, a poet's words could be read and enjoyed by people of many different backgrounds, when he wrote:

> Yet I doubt not through the ages one increasing purpose runs,
> And the thoughts of men are widened with the process of the suns.*

Whether or not the integration of culture which we construct retrospectively for these golden ages existed in actuality is an important question scientifically. But thinking about models, the question of actuality is less important. For the daydream and the vision, whether it was constructed by a prophet looking toward a new time or by a scholar working retrospectively, can still serve as a model of the future. Men may never, in fact, have attained the integration which some scholars believe characterized fifth-century Athens. Even so, their vision provides a chal-

*Alfred Tennyson, "Locksley Hall" (1842).

lenging picture of what might be attained by modern men who have so many possibilities for thinking about and for controlling the direction in which their culture will move.

However, all these models—as well as the simpler model of the pioneering American farmer, dressed in homespun, reared on the King James Version of the Bible, and sustained by simple foods and simple virtues—share one peculiarity. In each case the means of integration is a corpus of materials from the past. The epic poems of Homer, the Confucian classics, the Jewish and the Christian Scriptures—each of these, in giving the scholar and the man in the street, the playwright and the politician, access to an articulate statement of a world view, has been a source of integration. But the community of understanding of what was newly created—the poem, the play, the set of laws, the sculpture, the system of education, the style of landscape, the song—still depended on something which had been completed in the past. Today there is a continuing complaint that we have no such source of integration, and many of the measures which, it is suggested, would give a new kind of order to thinking are designed to provide just such a body of materials. There is, for example, the proposal to teach college students the history of science as a way of giving all of them access to the scientific view of the world. Or there is the related proposal to teach all students evolution, particularly the existing body of knowledge about the evolution of man and culture, as a way of providing a kind of unity within which all specialists, no matter how specialized, would have a common set of referents.

But such suggestions place too much reliance on the past and necessarily depend on a long time span within which to build a common, shared view of the world. In the present crisis the need to establish a shared body of assumptions is a very pressing one—too pressing to wait for the slow process of educating a small elite group in a few places in the world. The danger of nuclear disaster, which will remain with us even if all stockpiled bombs are destroyed, has created a hothouse atmosphere of crisis which forces a more rapid solution to our problems and at the same time wilts any solution which does not reflect this sense of urgency. For there is not only a genuine need for rapid solutions but also a growing restiveness among those who seek a solution. This restiveness in turn may well become a condition within which hasty, inadequate solutions are attempted—such as the substitution of slum pictures for ideal suburban middle-class pictures in slum children's textbooks—within too narrow a context. Speed in working out new solutions is essential if new and more disastrous fragmentations are not to occur—but we also need an appropriate framework.

Measures taken at the college level to establish mutual understanding between the natural scientist and the humanist, the social scientist and the administrator, men trained in the law and men trained in the behavioral sciences, have a double drawback. The cumulative effect of these measures would be too slow and, in addition, they would be inadequate in that their hope lies in establishing a corpus based on something which already exists—a theory of history, a history of science, or an account of evolution as it is now known. Given the changing state of knowledge in the modern world, any such historically based body of materials becomes in part out of date before it has been well organized and widely taught. Furthermore, it would be betrayed and diluted and corrupted by those who did the teaching, as they would inevitably have to draw on their own admittedly fragmented education to convey what was to be learned. One effect of this fragmentation can be seen in attempts to express forms of new knowledge in imagery which cannot contain it, because the imagery is shaped to an earlier view of the world. In a recent sermon, for example, the Bishop of Woolwich presented a picture of dazzling contemporaneity in disavowing the possibility of belief in the corporal ascension of Christ; but then, in proclaiming a new version of the Scriptures, he used the image of the sovereignty of Christ—an outmoded image in the terms in which he was speaking.

In the last hundred years men of science have fought uneasily with the problem of their own religious belief, and men of God have hardened their earlier visions into concrete images to confront a science they have not understood. Natural scientists have elaborated their hierarchical views of "true" science into an inability to understand the nature of the sciences of human behavior, welcoming studies of fragmented aspects of human behavior, or an inappropriate reduction in the number of variables. Human scientists have destroyed the delicacy and intricacy of their subject matter in coarse-grained attempts to imitate the experimental methods of Newtonian physics instead of developing new methods of including unanalyzable components in simulations or in developing new methods of validating the analysis of unique and complex historical events. As a result we lack the capacity to teach and the capacity to learn from a corpus based on the past. The success of any such venture would be comparably endangered by the past learning of the teachers and the past learning of the students, whose minds would already be formed by eighteen years of exposure to an internally inconsistent, contradictory, half-articulated, muddled view of the world.

But there is still another serious drawback to most current proposals for establishing mutual understanding. This is, in general, their lack of inclusiveness. Whether an approach to past knowledge is narrowly limited to the English-speaking world or includes the whole Euro-American tradition, whether it begins with the Greeks or extends backward in time to include the Paleolithic, any approach through the past can begin only with one sector of the world's culture. Inevitably, because of the historical separation of peoples and the diversity of the world's cultures throughout history, any one view of any one part of human tradition, based in the past, excludes other parts and, by emphasizing one aspect of human life, limits access to other aspects.

In the newly emerging nations we can see clearly the consequences of the efforts made by colonial educators to give to distant peoples a share in English or French or Dutch or Belgian or Spanish culture. Ironically, the more fully the colonial educators were willing to have some members at least of an African or an Asian society share in their traditions and their classics, the more keenly those who were so educated felt excluded from participation in the culture as a whole. For the classical European scholar, Africa existed mainly in very specialized historical contexts, and for centuries European students were concerned only with those parts of Africa or Asia which were ethnocentrically relevant to Greek or Roman civilization or the early Christian church. Throughout these centuries peoples without a written tradition and peoples with a separate written tradition (the Chinese, for example, or the Javanese) lived a life to which no one in Europe was related. With the widening of the European world in the fifteenth and sixteenth centuries, Europeans treated the peoples whom they "discovered" essentially as peoples without a past, except as the European connoisseur came to appreciate their monuments and archeological ruins, or later, as European students selectively used the histories of other peoples to illustrate their own conceptions of human history. Consequently, the greater degree of participation felt by the member of one of these more recently contacted societies in a French or an English view of the development of civilization, the more he also felt that his own cultural history was excluded from the history of man.

It is true that some heroic attempts have been made to correct this colonial bias. Looking at a synchronic table of events, a child anywhere in the world may set and ponder what the Chinese or the Mayans or the ancient canoe-sailing Hawaiians were doing when William the Conqueror landed in England. But almost inevitably this carefully constructed synchrony— with parallel columns of events for different parts of the world

—is undone, on the one hand, by the recognition that the New World and the Old, the Asian mainland and the Pacific islands, were not part of a consciously connected whole in A.D. 1066, and, on the other hand, by the implications of the date and the dating form, which carry the stamp of one tradition and one religious group within that tradition. It is all but impossible to write about the human past—the movements of early man, the building of the earliest known cities, the spread of artifacts and art forms, the development of styles of prophecy or symbolism —without emphasizing how the spirit of man has flowered at different times in different places and, time and again, in splendid isolation. Even in this century, the efforts of scholars to integrate the histories of the world's great living traditions have led, in the end, to a renewed preoccupation with each of these as an entity with its own long history.

Today, however, if we are to construct the beginning of a shared culture, using every superior instrument at our command and with full consciousness both of the hazards and the possibilities, we can stipulate certain properties which this still nonexistent corpus must have.

It must be equally suitable for all peoples from whatever traditions their present ways of living spring, and it must not give undue advantage to those peoples anywhere in the world whose traditions have been carried by a longer or a more fully formulated literacy. While those who come from a culture with a Shakespeare or a Dante will themselves be the richer, communications should not be so laden with allusions to Shakespeare or Dante that those who lack such a heritage cannot participate. Nor should the wealth of perceptual verbal detail in distinguishing colors, characteristic of the Dusun of Borneo or the Hanunoo of the Philippines, be used to make less differentiated systems seem crude. The possession of a script for a generation, a century, or a millennium must be allowed for in ways that will make it possible for all peoples to start their intercommunication on a relatively equal basis. No single geographical location, no traditional view of the universe, no special set of figures of speech, by which one tradition but not another has been informed, can provide an adequate base. It must be such that everyone, everywhere, can start afresh, as a young child does, with a mind ready to meet ideas uncompromised by partial learning. It must be cast in a form that does not depend on years of previous learning—the fragmented learning already acquired by the college student or the student in the high school, the lycée, or the gymnasium. Instead, it must be cast in a form that is appropriate for small children—for children whose fathers are shepherds, rubber tappers in jungles, forgotten sharecroppers, sailors or fishermen, miners or members of the dispossessed urban proletariat, as well as for the children whose forebears have read one of the world's scripts for many generations.

If this body of materials on which a new, shared culture is to be based is to include all the peoples of the world, then the peoples of the world must also contribute to it in ways that are qualitatively similar. If it is to escape from the weight of discrepant centuries, the products of civilization included within it must be chosen with the greatest care. The works of art must be universal in their appeal and examples of artistic endeavor whose processes are universally available—painting, drawing, carving, dancing, and singing in forms that are universally comprehensible. Only after a matrix of shared understanding has been developed will the way be prepared for the inclusion of specific, culturally separate traditions. But from the first it must have the character of a living tradition, so it will be free of the static qualities of older cultures, with texts that have become the test of truth and forms so rigid that experimentation has become impossible. And it must have the qualities of a natural language, polished and pruned and capable of expansion by the efforts of many minds of different calibres, redundant and sufficiently flexible so it will meet the needs of teacher and pupil, parent and child, friend and friend, master and apprentice, lawyer and client, statesman and audience, scientist and humanist, in their different modes of communication. It is through use in all the complexity of relationships like these that a natural language is built and, given form and content by many kinds of human beings, becomes a medium of communication that can be learned by every child, however slight its natural ability. This projected corpus should not be confused with present-day popular culture, produced commercially with contempt for its consumers. Instead, by involving the best minds, the most sensitive and gifted artists and poets and scientists, the new shared culture should have something of the quality of the periods of folk tradition out of which great art has repeatedly sprung.

A body of materials having these characteristics must bear the imprint of growth and use. Yet it is needed now, in this century, for children who are already born and for men who either will preserve the world for a new generation to grow up in or who, in failing to do so, will doom the newly interconnected peoples of the world to destruction by means of the very mechanisms which have made a world community a possibility. The most immediate problem, then, is that of producing, almost overnight, a corpus which expresses and makes possible new processes of growth.

We believe that the existing state of our knowledge about the process of consciousness is such that it is necessary for us only to ask the right questions in order to direct our thinking toward answers. Today engineering and the technology of applied physical science have outstripped other applied sciences because in these fields searching questions have been asked urgently, sharply, and insistently. This chapter is an attempt to ask questions, set up a series of specifications, and illustrate the order of answer for which we should be looking. There will be better ways of formulating these questions, all of which have to do with communication, and better ways of meeting the criteria which will make answers possible. In fact, it is my assumption that the creation of a body of materials which will serve our needs will depend on the contribution and the participation of all those who will also further its growth, that is, people in every walk of life, in every part of the globe, speaking every language and seeing the universe in the whole range of forms conceived by man.

The Future as a Setting

I would propose that we consider the future as the appropriate setting for our shared worldwide culture, for the future is least compromised by partial and discrepant views. And I would choose the near future over the far future, so as to avoid as completely as possible new confusions based on partial but avowedly totalistic projections born of the ideologies of certainty, like Marxism and Leninism, or the recurrent scientific dogmatisms about the possibilities of space travel, the state of the atmosphere, or the appearance of new mutations. But men's divergent dreams of eternity might be left undisturbed, providing they did not include some immediate apocalyptic moment for the destruction of the world.

Looking toward the future, we would start to build from the known. In many cases, of course, this would be knowledge very newly attained. What we would build on, then, would be the known attributes of the universe, our solar system, and the place of our earth within this system; the known processes of our present knowledge, from which we shall proceed to learn more; the known treasures of man's plastic and graphic genius as a basis for experience out of which future artists may paint and carve, musicians compose, and poets speak; the known state of instrumentation, including both the kinds of instrumentation which have already been developed (for example, communication satellites) and those which are ready to be developed; the known numbers of human beings, speaking a known number of languages, and living in lands with known amounts of fertile soil, fresh water, and irreplaceable natural resources; the known forms of organizing men into functioning groups; and the known state of modern weaponry, with its known capacity to destroy all life.

These various kinds of knowledge would be viewed as beginnings, instead of as ends—as young, growing forms of knowledge, instead of as finished products to be catalogued, diagrammed, and preserved in the pages of encyclopedias. All statements would take the form: "We know that there are at least X number of stars" (or people in Asia, or developed forms of transporation, or forms of political organization). Each such statement would be phrased as a starting point—a point from which to move onward. In this sense the great artistic productions of all civilizations could be included, not as the splendid fruit of one or another civilization, but on new terms, as points of departure for the imagination.

The frenetic, foolhardy shipping of original works of art around the world in ships and planes, however fragile they may be, can be looked upon as a precursor of this kind of change— as tales of flying saucers preceded man's first actual ventures into space. It is as if we already dimly recognized that if we are to survive, we must share all we have, at whatever cost, so that men everywhere can move toward some as yet undefined taking-off point into the future.

But if we can achieve a new kind of consciousness of what we are aiming at, we do not need actually to move these priceless objects as if they were figures in a dream. We can, instead, take thought how, with our modern techniques, we can make the whole of an art style available, not merely single, symbolic examples, torn from their settings. Young painters and poets and musicians, dancers and architects, can today be given access to all that is known about color and form, perspective and rhythm, technique and the development of style, the relationships of form and style and material, and the interrelationships of art forms as these have been developed in some place, at some time. We have all the necessary techniques to do this. We can photograph in color, train magnifying cameras on the inaccessible details of domes and towers, record a poet reciting his own poetry, film an artist as he paints, and use film and sound to transport people from any one part to any other part of the world to participate in the uncovering of an ancient site or the first viewing of a new dance form. We can, in fact, come out of the "manuscript stage" for all the arts, for process as well as product, and make the whole available simultaneously to a young generation so they can move ahead together and congruently into the future. Given access to the range of the world's art, young artists can see in a new light those special activities and art objects to which they themselves are immediately related, wherever they are.

Working always within the modest limits of one generation —the next twenty-five years—and without tempting the massive consequences of miscalculation, we can include the known aspects of the universe in which our continuing experimental ventures into space will be conducted and the principles, the tools, and the materials with which these ventures are beginning. Children all over the world can be given accurate, tangible models of what we now know about the solar system, models of the earth, showing how it is affected by the large-scale patterning of weather, and models showing how life on earth may be affected by events in the solar system and beyond. Presented with a clear sense of the expanding limits of our knowledge, models such as these would prepare children everywhere to participate in discoveries we know must come and to anticipate new aspects of what is as yet unknown.

Within these same limits we can bring together our existing knowledge of the world's multitudes—beginning with those who are living now and moving out toward those who will be living twenty-five years from now. The world is well mapped, and we know, within a few millions, how many people there are, where they are, and who they are. We know—or have the means of knowing—a great deal about the world's peoples. We know about the world's food supplies and can relate our knowledge to the state of those who have been well nourished and those who have been poorly fed. We know about the world's health and can relate our knowledge to the state of those who have been exposed to ancient plagues and those who are exposed to "modern" ambiguous viruses. We can picture the ways of living of those who, as children, were reared in tents, in wattle and daub houses, in houses made of mud bricks, in tenements and apartment houses, in peasant houses that have survived unchanged through hundreds of years of occupancy and in the new small houses of modern suburbs, in the anonymity of urban housing, in isolated villages, and in the crowded shacks of refugee settlements. We can define the kinds of societies, all of them contemporary, in which human loyalties are restricted to a few hundred persons, all of them known to one another, and others in which essential loyalties are expanded to include thousands or millions or even hundreds of millions of persons, only a few of them known to one another face to face. In the past we could, at best, give children some idea of the world's multitudes through books, printed words, and meager illustrations. Today we have the resources to give children everywhere living experience of the whole contemporary world. And every child, everywhere in the world, can start with that knowledge and grow into its complexity. In this way plans for population control, flood control, control of man's inroads on nature, plans for protecting human health and for developing a world food supply, and plans for sharing a world communication system can all become plans in which citizens participate in informed decisions.

None of this knowledge will in any sense be ultimate. We do

not know what form knowledge itself will take twenty-five years from now, but we do know what its sources must be in present knowledge and, ordering what we now know, we can create a ground plan for the future on which all the peoples of the earth can build.

Because it must be learned by very young children and by the children of very simple parents, this body of knowledge and experience must be expressed in clear and simple terms, using every graphic device available to us and relying more on models than on words, for in many languages appropriate words are lacking. The newer and fresher the forms of presentation are, the greater will be the possibility of success, for, as in the new mathematics teaching, all teachers—those coming out of old traditions and having long experience with special conventions and those newly aware of the possibilities of formal teaching— will have to learn what they are to teach as something new. Furthermore, parents will be caught up in the process, in one sense as the pupils of their children, discovering that they can reorder their own knowledge and keep the pace, and in another sense as supplementary teachers, widening the scope of teaching and learning. Knowledge arranged for comprehensibility by a young child is knowledge accessible to all, and the task of arranging it will necessarily fall upon the clearest minds in every field of the humanities, the sciences, the arts, engineering, and politics.

There is, however, one very immediate question. How are we to meet the problem of shared contribution? How are we to ensure that this corpus is not in the end a simplified version of modern Western—essentially Euro-American—scientific and philosophic thought and of art forms and processes, however widely selected, interpreted within the Western tradition? Is there any endeavor which can draw on the capacities not only of those who are specially trained but also those with untapped resources—the uneducated in Euro-American countries and the adult and wise in old, exotic cultures and newly emerging ones?

A first answer can be found, I think, in activities in which every country can have a stake and persons of every age and level of sophistication can take part. One such activity would be the fashioning of a new set of communication devices—like the visual device used by very simple peoples to construct messages or to guide travelers on their way, but now raised to the level of worldwide intelligibility.

In recent years there has been extensive discussion of the need for a systematic development of what are now called glyphs, that is, graphic representations, each of which stands for an idea: male, female, water, poison, danger, stop, go, etc. Hundreds of glyphs are used in different parts of the world—as road signs, for example—but too often with ambiguous or contradictory meanings as one moves from one region to another. What is needed, internationally, is a set of glyphs which does not refer to any single phonological system or to any specific cultural system of images but will, instead, form a system of visual signs with universally recognized referents. But up to the present no sustained effort has been made to explore the minimum number that would be needed or to make a selection that would carry clear and unequivocal meaning for the peoples of the world, speaking all languages, living in all climates, and exposed to very different symbol systems. A project for the exploration of glyph forms and for experimentation with the adequacy of different forms has been authorized by the United Nations Committee for International Cooperation Year (1965). This is designed as an activity in which adults and children, artists and engineers, logicians and semanticists, linguists and historians— all those, in fact, who have an interest in doing so—can take part. For the wider the range of persons and the larger the number of cultures included in this exploration, the richer and the more fully representative will be the harvest from which a selection of glyphs can be made for international use.

Since meaning is associated with each glyph as a unit and glyphs cannot be combined syntactically, they can be used by the speakers of any language. But considerable experimentation will be necessary to avoid ambiguity which may lead to confusion or the adoption of forms which are already culturally loaded. The variety of meanings which may already be associated with certain forms can be illustrated by the sign + (which, in different connections, can be the sign for addition or indicate a positive number, can stand for "north" or indicate a crossroad, and, very slightly modified, can indicate a deceased person in a genealogy, a specifically Christian derivation, or stand for the Christian sign of the cross), or the sign O (which, in different connections, may stand for circumference or for 360°, for the full moon, for an annual plant, for degrees of arc or temperature, for an individual, especially female, organism, and very slightly modified, can stand for zero or, in our alphabet, the letter O).

Work on glyphs can lead to work on other forms of international communication. In an interconnected world we shall need a world language—a second language which could be learned by every people but which would in no sense replace their native tongue. Contemporary studies of natural languages have increased our understanding of the reasons why consciously constructed languages do not serve the very complex purposes of general communication. Most important is the fact that an artificial language, lacking the imprint of many different kinds of minds and differently organized capacities for response, lacks the redundancy necessary in a language all human beings can learn.

Without making any premature choice, we can state some of the criteria for such a secondary world language. It must be a natural language, chosen from among known living languages, but not from among those which are today politically controversial. Final choice would depend also on the outcome of systematic experiments with mechanical translation, and so on. In addition, it would be essential to consider certain characteristics related to the current historical situation. Politically, it should be the language of a state too small to threaten other states. In order to allow for a rapid development of diverse written styles, it must be a language with a long tradition of use in written form. To permit rapid learning, it must be a language whose phonetic system can be easily learned by speakers of other languages, and one which can be easily rendered into a phonetic script and translated without special difficulty into existing traditional scripts. It should come from the kind of population in which there is a wide diversity of roles and occupations and among whom a large number of teachers can be found, some of whom are already familiar with one or another of the great widespread languages of the world. Using modern methods of language teaching, the task of creating a worldwide body of readers and speakers could be accomplished within five years and the language itself would change in the process of this worldwide learning.

If a secondary world language were to be chosen, the body of knowledge with which we could start the next twenty-five years could be translated into it from preliminary statements in the great languages, taking the stamp of these languages as divergent subtleties of thought, present in one language and absent in another, were channeled in a new vocabulary created to deal with new ideas.

One important effect of a secondary world language would be to protect the more localized languages from being swamped by those few which are rapidly spreading over the world. Plans have been advanced to make possible the learning and use of any one of the five or seven most widespread languages as a second language. Fully implemented, this would divide the world community into two classes of citizens—those for whom one of these languages was a mother tongue and those for whom it was a second language—and it would exacerbate already existing problems arising from differences in the quality of communication—rapid and idiomatic among native speakers and slower, more formal, and less spontaneous among those who have learned English, French, or Russian later. In contrast, one shared second language, used on a worldwide scale, would tend to equalize the quality of world communication and at the same time would protect the local diversity of all other languages.

Another important aspect of a shared culture would be the articulate inclusion of the experience of those who travel to study, work, explore, or enjoy other countries. One of the most intractable elements in our present isolating cultures is the interlocking of a landscape—a landscape with mountains or a desert, jungle or tundra, rushing cataracts or slow-flowing rivers, arched over by a sky in which the Dipper or the Southern Cross dominates—and a view of man. The beauty of face and movement of those who have never left their mountains or their island is partly the imprint on the human form of a complex relationship to the scale and the proportions, the seasonal rhythms and the natural style, of one special part of the world. The experiences of those who have been bred to one physical environment cannot be patched together like the pieces of a patchwork quilt. But we can build on the acute and vivid experiences of those who, reared in a culture which has incorporated its environment, can respond to the countryman as to the city dweller; the response of the city dweller to open country, the response of the immigrant to the sweep of an untouched landscape and of the traveler to a sudden vista into the past of a whole people. In the past the visual impact of discovery was recorded retrospectively in painting and in literature. Today films can record the more immediate response of the observer, looking with fresh eyes at the world of the nomadic Bushman or the people beneath the mountain wall of New Guinea, at the palaces in Crete or the summer palace in Peking.

We can give children a sense of movement, actually experienced or experienced only in some leap of the imagination. In the next twenty-five years we shall certainly not explore deep space, but the experience of movement can link a generation in a common sense of anticipation. As a beginning we can give children a sense of different actual relationships to the physical environments of the whole earth, made articulate through the recorded responses of those who have moved from one environment to another. Through art, music, and film we can give children access to the ways others have experienced their own green valleys and other valleys, also green. We can develop in small children the capacity to wonder and to look through other eyes at the familiar fir trees rimming their horizon or the sea breaking on their island's shore.

In the past these have been the experiences of those who could afford to travel and those who had access, through the arts, to the perceptions of a poet like Wordsworth in "The Prelude," or a young scientist like Darwin on his Pacific voyage, or painters like Catlin or Gauguin. With today's technology these need no longer be the special experiences of the privileged and the educated elite. The spur to action may be the desire for literacy in the emerging nations or a new concern for the culturally deprived in older industrialized countries. And quite different styles of motivation can give urgency to the effort to bring the experience of some to bear on the experience of all.

Looking to the future, the immediacy of motivation is itself part of the experience. It may be an assertive desire to throw off a colonial past or a remorseful attempt to atone for long neglect. It may be the ecumenical spirit in which Pope John XXIII can say: "No pilgrim, no matter how far, religiously and geographically, may be the country from which he comes, will be any longer a stranger to this Rome. . . ." It may be the belief that it is possible to remake a society, as when Martin Luther King said:*

> I have a dream today . . . I have a dream that one day every valley shall be exalted, every hill and mountain shall be made low. The rough places will be made plain, and the crooked places will be made straight. And the glory of the Lord shall be revealed, and all flesh shall see it together. This is our hope. This is the faith that I go back to the South with. With this faith we will be able to hew out of the mountain of despair a stone of hope.

Or it may be the belief, expressed by U Thant,** that men can work toward a world society:

> Let us look inward for a moment and recognize that no one, no individual, no nation, and indeed no ideology has a monopoly of rightness, freedom or dignity. And let us translate this recognition into action so as to sustain the fullness and freedom of simple human relations leading to ever widening areas of understanding and agreement. Let us, on this day, echo the wish which Rabindranath Tagore stated in these memorable words, so that our world may be truly a world
> Where the mind is without fear and the head is held high;
> Where knowledge is free;
> Where the world has not been broken up into fragments by narrow domestic walls;
> Where words come out of the depth of truth;
> Where tireless striving stretches its arms toward perfection . . .

There are also other ways in which experience can more consciously be brought to bear in developing a shared understanding. All traditions, developing slowly over centuries, are shaped by the biological nature of man—the differences in temperament and constitution among men and processes of matu-

*From the speech by the Rev. Martin Luther King at the March on Washington, *New York Post Magazine*, September 1, 1963, p. 5.
**From the Human Rights Day Message by (then) Acting Secretary-General U Thant, December 8, 1961.

ration, parenthood, and aging which are essential parts of our humanity. The conscious inclusion of the whole life process in our thinking can, in turn, alter the learning process, which in a changing world has become deeply disruptive as each elder generation has been left behind while the next has been taught an imperfect version of the new. One effect of this has been to alienate and undermine the faith of parents and grandparents as they have seen their children's minds moving away from them and as their own beliefs, unshared, have become inflexible and distorted.

The policy in most of today's world is to educate the next—the new—generation, setting aside the older generation in the mistaken hope that, as older men and women are passed over, their outmoded forms of knowledge will do no harm. Instead, we pay a double price in the alienation of the new generation from their earliest and deepest experiences as little children and in the blocking of constructive change in the world by an older generation who still exercise actual power—hoarding some resources and wasting others, building to an outmoded scale, voting against measures the necessity of which is not understood, supporting reactionary leaders, and driving an equally inflexible opposition toward violence. Yet this lamentable outcome was unnecessary.

In the past the transmission of the whole body of knowledge within a slowly changing society has provided for continuity. Today we need to create an educational style which will provide for continuity and openness even within rapid change. Essentially this means an educational style in which members of different generations are involved in the process of learning. One way of assuring this is through a kind of education in which new things are taught to mothers and young children together. The mothers, however schooled, usually are less affected by contemporary styles of education than the fathers. In some countries they have had no schooling; in others, girls are

warned away from science and mathematics or even from looking at the stars. So they come to the task of rearing their small
children fresher than those who have been trained to teach or
to administer. Child rearing in more than the past fifty years has
been presented as almost entirely a matter of molding the emo-
tional life of the child, modulating the effects of demands for
cleanliness and obedience to permit more spontaneity, and of
preserving an environment in which there is good nutrition and
low infection danger. At the same time we have taken out of the
hands of mothers the education even of young children. So we
have no existing rationale in which mother, child, and teacher
are related within the learning process. What we need now in
every part of the world is a new kind of school for mothers and
little children in which mothers learn to teach children what
neither the mothers nor the children know.

Then we may ask, are such plans as these sufficiently open-
ended? In seeking to make equally available to the peoples of
the world newly organized ways of moving into the immediate
future, in a universe in which our knowledge is rapidly expanding, there is always the danger that the idea of a shared body
of knowledge may be transformed into some kind of universal
blueprint. In allowing this to happen we would, of course, de-
feat our own purpose. The danger is acute enough so that we
must build a continuing wariness and questioning into the planning itself; otherwise even the best plan may result in a closed
instead of an open-ended system.

This means that we must be open-ended in our planning as
well as our plans, recognizing that this will involve certain kinds
of conscious restructure as well as conscious questioning. We
must insist on the inclusion of peoples from all over the world
in any specific piece of planning—as in the development of an
international system of glyphs—as a way of assuring a growing
and an unpredictable corpus. We must be willing to forego, in
large-scale planning, some kinds of apparent efficiency. If we

are willing, instead, to include numerous steps and to conceive of each step somewhat differently, we are more likely, in the end, to develop new interrelationships, unforeseeable at any early stage. A more conscious inclusion of women and of the grandparental generation in learning and teaching will carry with it the extraordinary differences in existing interrelations between the minds and in the understanding of the two sexes and different age groups.

We can also take advantage of what has been learned through the use of culture which we are launching with a system of multiple self-corrective devices. For example, criteria could be established for reviewing the kinds of divergences that were occurring in vocabulary and conceptualizations as an idea fanned out around the world. Similarly, the rate and type of incorporation of special developments in particular parts of the world could be monitored, and cases of dilution or distortion examined and corrected. Overemphasis on one part of knowledge, on one sensory modality, on the shells men live in rather than the life they live there, on sanitation rather than beauty, on length of life rather than quality of life lived, could be listened for and watched for, and corrective measures taken speedily.

A special area of concern would be intercommunication among all those whose specializations tend to isolate them from one another, scientist from administrator, poet from statesman, citizen voter from the highly skilled specialist who must carry out his mandate using calculations which the voter cannot make, but within a system of values clearly enough stated so that both may share them. By attending to the origins of some new communication—whether a political, a technical, or an artistic innovation—the functioning of the communication process could be monitored. Special sensing organs could be established which would observe, record, and correct so that what otherwise might become a blundering, linear, and unmanageable avalanche could be shaped into a process delicately responsive to change in itself.

But always the surest guarantee of change and growth is the inconclusion of living persons in every stage of an activity. Their lives, their experience, and their continuing response—even their resistances—infuse with life any plan which, if living participants are excluded, lies on the drawing board and loses its reality. Plans for the future can become old before they are lived, but the future itself is always newborn and, like any newborn thing, is open to every kind of living experience.

XI Promise
(1971)

I believe that we should substitute for the present tendency to characterize technologies and social arrangements which draw upon science, as *rational*, and those assumptions and practices which draw upon the arts, the great religions, and the active commitment of groups of men to the perpetuation of their historical cultures, as *irrational*. This introduces a dichotomy which disallows depths of emotion, the potentialities of artistic expression, and the vigor of action which has been associated through time with love of country and commitment to succeeding generations. I believe that instead of dichotomizing human social behavior, in such matters as the protection of our endangered planetary environment, or the attainment of a balanced degree of population increase, or the reduction of armaments which by their very existence threaten the survival of mankind, we should speak not of *rational* as over against *irrational* measures, but instead, of *responsible* as over against *irresponsible* measures. Under the word *responsible* I would group the use of the best scientific knowledge and the best available techniques, the invocation of deep feeling and the fire that can be provided by devotion to kin and country, forebears and descendants, the close and dear association with contemporaries and colleagues, the inspiring realization of the oneness of mankind, and action powered by this combination of knowledge and sentiment. Only so can we see that there is no necessary opposition between our historical sentiments of deep unanalyzable devotion to our own ways of life and the need for worldwide cooperation in common and terribly urgent tasks. Science and technology based upon scientific discoveries have now provided us with a new means for realizing man's most ancient needs for survival, as groups of identifiable human beings, and those who embody traditions developed through centuries of human effort, the inspired imagination of genius, and the suffering and endurance of countless generations. Today we can feed the hungry, shelter the homeless, protect our children while they sleep, and create conditions in which every child born will be a wanted child, given a full chance as an individual and as a potential contributor to our common human cultural and biological heritage. We now have the means to do these things. The knowledge that we have these means, even more than the exposure of the suffering and disadvantaged peoples to the sight of abundance and affluence, has given rise to the great surge of hope throughout the world. But it has also provided a rationale for despair, as people see their own countries or their own fellows sunk in sloughs of deprivation which can no longer be defined as the inevitable consequence of our humanity. In the fever heat of alternating hope and despair, a mere call to the rational disposition of irreplaceable natural resources, the protection of the environment against irreversible deterioration, the establishment of population balance in the face of runaway population increase, is not enough. Recognition of the necessities for such rational action, that is, of the utilization of the findings of science and the capacities of modern technology, is not enough. Genuine passion, the passion that comes from man's deepest and earliest commitments, must be invoked and embodied in action, visible, palpable, dramatic, and standing as living witness to a wider, and deeper, concern for the whole and for each precious part, each language, each cherished belief, each cluster of living human beings, united to each other in communities so organically related that tearing them apart is like tearing apart the organs of a living body. Our action, at once informed and passionate, must include not only concern for each living human being, and for each living tradition, but also for each living community. Each year of experience in the great adventure of making an intercommunicating and mutually endangered set of once separate societies into a worldwide community brings us new insight into the requirements of the tasks ahead. We have reached the point where each country is endangered by any disaster to any one of the other countries on this planet, but we have yet to translate this frightening interdependence into the kind of relationships which provide security and joy in living and acceptance of sacrifice even unto death which have been previously provided in separate cultures.

I wish to outline a few of the ways in which I believe we can improve our efforts to establish such a world culture. But first I wish to emphasize that I am not urging a world state, as the model of the state inevitably included a position vis-à-vis one or more other nation-states, in uneasy coexistence, or muted hostility and rivalry. On our small and endangered planet, the continued existence of opposed segments is a poor solution to the problems of survival. Nor can a planet, isolated in our solar system, however much it may be one of many inhabited stars throughout the galaxies, depend upon an organization primarily designed to protect against enemies, and almost inevitably leading to competition for hegemony and invitations to revolt. I believe that we need better models than the nation-state, and better models than federation of previously sovereign national units. We have yet to develop such a model in which activities, rather than spatial entities, which are bounded and mutually exclusive, can be interwoven over the surface of the globe, transcending other lines of allegiance and participation. But we have faint beginnings of such networks in the way in which the different members of the United Nations system are located in different countries, and represent both the attempt to satisfy universal needs and the unique capacity of single great cultures: France for the United Nations Educational, Scientific & Cultural Organization, Switzerland for the World Health Organization, Austria for the International Atomic Energy Agency, Italy for the Food and Agriculture Organization, are united in efforts to meet some of the recognized needs of mankind. Internationally organized economic enterprises, and internationally organized groups of workers, provide other partial models of the way in which a mesh of institutional solutions to the worldwide human needs might be established, within which the conflicts between the center and the periphery common to all present forms of organization could be mitigated by the distribution of many centers in different parts of the world, each a center for one of the universal needs of mankind, essential to the whole, but unable to satisfy that need alone without the other institutions organized to meet other needs. To date our political imaginations have been shackled by historical models of empires, nation-states, centralized and stratified bureaucracies, all of which have arisen during a period when the planet was divided up among many peoples who only intermittently communicated with one another. None of them are appropriate for an explored, owned, and shared planet on whose continued fertility and beneficent waters and sheltering atmosphere we are all dependent.

I shall now turn to more specific and narrower tasks. I believe we need to inventory all of these dimensions of the physical universe, on the accurate measurement of which the achievements of science and science-based technology depend: weight, length, volume, units of time and space, and units of artificial constructs like currency, architecture, and engineering. It is absolutely essential that a single system of measurement and symbolization be used around the world. Significantly, there is no need for continuous simultaneous translation in the international congresses in those physical sciences where the agreed-upon sets of symbols are used worldwide. It is necessary to extend these systems, steadily, to every field of science and science-based technology. In anthropology I would mention particularly the need of an agreed-upon geophysical calendar, to use as a base and a point of reference for the various calendars now used in different cultures, and the need for a culture-free terminology to describe human beings' biological relationships, presently described in ethnocentric abbreviations of English kinship terms. A failure to make such world-wide sets of symbols, freed from cultural particulars, immensely hampers the spread of scientific knowledge and science-based technologies, emphasizes and exacerbates the worst aspects of nationalistic chauvinism, and imposes huge economic burdens on many parts of the world. The failure of the United States and the United Kingdom to adopt the metric system when it was invented is a case in point, as is the insistence of different nations upon calendars based on the birth of a prophet of the dominant religion or on events in their own political history. All of these can be preserved for ceremonial internal use, as archaic technology is preserved within meaningful religious and political rituals, while a worldwide and rationalized terminological system continually expands, as our ability to measure different aspects of reality increases with the advance of science from measurement of physical events to the measurement of human behavior. Every year that such rationalization is delayed puts a greater burden upon mankind's ability to use scientific findings for human ends.

We need to invent a written language which is independent both of existing scripts and existing spoken languages, which gives no special advantage to the linguistic style of any part of the world, which permits the visual presentation of ideas, in the same way as Chinese script transcends the different spoken languages of China. The availability of closed-circuit television means that with such a new written language, complex ideas could be communicated, without the need for laborious and inexact and approximate translations, to groups who differ profoundly in language and culture.

Such a written language, which would have no single equivalence in words, needs to be complemented by a shared spoken language which can be learned as a second language by an increasing number of the world's people. Such a language should not draw on any linguistic area of the world in a way which would give any group an advantage, and it should be based on a natural language, which has itself been adapted through centuries of use to the needs and capacities of men, clever and stupid, profound and shallow-minded, as spoken by the childish, the senile, and even the mad, as well as by poets and songmakers and philosophers.

Only by developing universal symbolic communication independent of any present spoken language, and a second spoken language with an appropriate form of script, can we hope to preserve the little as well as the widespread languages of the world. Without it, the widespread languages will contend together for victory, and those who speak less widespread languages will be condemned to second-class linguistic citizenry, struggling always a step behind the native speakers of the "official languages" of international communication. Only by insisting upon the development of two such forms of communication can we prevent grievous injustice and inequalities, and preserve the precious capacity for intimacy and poetry and religion which are so intricately related to the mother tongue, the language learned in infancy.

We need to find ways to express comparisons between achievements of nation-states, or subdivisions of nation-states, in ways which are less gross and invidious than statements about literacy or gross national product or rate of population increase. The significance of such measures is obscured when nations or cities are placed on single scales, so that they appear to be arrayed in hierarchical sets of superiority and inferiority. We need instead measures which reflect the complexity of each culture, the way in which the level of education is related to the demands for that education, the rate of population increase to maintaining a balance between the number of young and the number of skilled elders necessary to care for them and teach them, and the way in which such a ratio of youth to age is itself related to the natural resources of a country. Ratios which reflect types of internal balance or internal change themselves very different in detail would provide less invidious bases for comparisons, and would emphasize variety rather than uniformity of technical and social solutions.

As the process of urbanization spreads over the world, as men forsake the isolation of rural living which has been the accepted life-style of the majority of men since the agricultural revolution made it possible to live a settled life, we need new ways of balancing the importance of the small, interdependent community, larger than the family and smaller than a city, in which children can be reared to be full citizens and old people find again the small scale which they knew in childhood, where the adolescents and the mature, wearied by the impersonality of the modern rationalized forms of education and work, may return at nightfall to the many-dimensional satisfactions of a known and cherished human scale. In our search for mobility we have reduced life to too small units, to the single family of parents and children, a unit marvelously adapted to the exploitation of man by man, in soulless systems of production and consumption, in which each fragile household becomes dependent upon large-scale industrial and political bureaucracies. We need, in the greatly accelerated planning and construction of new cities and the replanning of old cities, to construct new urban systems in which small face-to-face communities can be maintained and where the countryside and the wilderness may be again accessible to man. Such communities need not become the static, self-perpetuating villages of the past and old rivalries and old expectations limited and defined the scope of each individual's ambitions. They can be open, based upon choice rather than biological kinship and occupational imperatives as in the past, and still provide the security and diversity of personal relationships once provided by the wider kinship group and the small village.

But as we redesign space to match the opportunity provided by modern methods of transportation and communication, we must also come to transcend space as the regulator of our political relationships and our capacity for shared activity. The new realization which has come with frightening suddenness, that air and water are also limited, and may be irreversibly damaged so that the planet becomes uninhabitable, has given us, with its new sense of limitation, new possibilities for the elimination of warfare and for worldwide cooperation. As long as our major concern was for space, for the establishment and the maintenance of boundaries, there seemed no reliable basis for worldwide cooperation among peoples. Each group's gain was another group's loss as the struggle for absolute sovereignty over territory ranged back and forth through the ages. The size of the units changed but the nature of the struggle did not. Two men cannot stand on the same space, two nations cannot exercise exclusive sovereignty over the same territory. But now that exploration and the scientific analysis of outer and inner space have brought us to a fuller understanding of the nature of the atmospheric shield which protects this planet, and the function of the great oceans in keeping it at a temperature that makes life possible, suddenly the very limitation which on the ground seemed to make conflict inevitable has released man to recognize a genuinely shared and common life-giving heritage of air and water. Just because of the fragility of the whole life-support system of this small planet, we now know that we are bound together in a common fate, long proclaimed by prophets and poets, now for the first time spelled out for us by the painstaking and breathtaking advances of science.

Far from setting up an opposition between science and the older, deeper commitments of man to love, to religion, to passion, to joy, and to sacrifices, these new realizations make their attainment more possible. In the past the only way in which we could extend the taboo against killing a member of one's own group was by increasing the size of the group itself, at the expense of other groups, until huge states of many millions confronted each other, each protecting its own millions against the millions of another state defined as predators or prey, beyond the limits of human brotherhood. Today, with air and water which we now know not only can be, but must be regarded as, the common possession of the whole of mankind if any group is to survive, the old imperatives of territoriality become the ground upon which we stand as we share and protect an atmosphere and oceans held in common.

Even as we cherish the differences in the historic traditions of each people, we can recognize that while the past of peoples who were bound to small parts of an unexplored and unrealized planet separated them one from another, the future, as yet uncharted, unsung, the property of no single nation, dependent upon our planetary ability to protect our earth, can unite us. Just at the moment when the tremendous advances in knowledge and the extraordinary extensions of planetary communication and space exploration seem to have introduced a terrible division between the elders, born into a divided, earthbound, tradition-limited world, and the young, who have lived intimately with the earth seen from the moon, seemed to threaten the necessary continuities of the whole of our society, this vision of our small and fragile planet has instead provided a sense of the future which old and young can share. I believe it is possible to cherish the past, to save our own special and diverse traditions, our mother tongues, and our culturally specialized aesthetic styles and religious visions, and the different symbols which have united men born in the same period and still bind the generations together, if we lay enough emphasis on that which all these divided groups share, a future to which we must all commit ourselves, in interdependence on our small and precious earth.

XII Celebration: A Human Need
(1968)

Americans, especially young Americans, are crying out for shared delight, for shared celebration of joy. This cry is expressed in many ways: by high school classes studying books about the rites of spring or puberty among primitive peoples, by lively young staffs of public parks looking for "happenings," by the counterpoint at a conference on church and society where a dancer is introduced to accentuate a Scriptural reading, followed by the singing of "I am the Lord of the Dance." Why, ask those arranging a love-in or planning to perch with their guitars on the edge of a heavy marble altar, can't we have more celebrations, more fresh, invigorating group events?

The demand is there, the imagination is there. But perhaps there is an unrecognized block to working out in a continuing and satisfying form the celebrations so earnestly and clamorously desired. One of the ways by which we can escape the narrow cultural walls that confine us (walls which do not yield to head knocking or breast beating or wailing) is to look at what other times and other peoples have made of celebrations, especially those peoples for whom annual or occasional ceremonies provide the principal focus of living. When we look at traditional societies—like Bali, for example—we find that celebration is inseparable from ritual. Highly stylized activities, repeated from celebration to celebration, from procession to procession, from year to year, are an essential part of the whole. Each large event may allow ample room for new elements, new songs, new drama, new costumes, new skits on the current world; but nevertheless the element of ritual, of sanctioned and valued repetition, is always there. Improvisation is possible because it can be done within a known and valued frame. New dances built on old dances: the drama of younger brother who always defeats his stupid and pompous older brother in the Balinese theater is always fresh and new because the performer is free—within an old, loved, tried form—to be fresh and contemporary.

Ritual, a repetition of recognized forms of expression, cannot be relegated to the past—to antiquity, to barbarism, or to the life of early man. Ritual is an exceedingly important part of all culture, all the cultures we now know about and, I would hope, all the cultures that will be known in the future.

Contemporary American celebrations suffer from our objection to anything we can classify as ritualistic, repetitive, or even familiar. Some of the roots of this attitude go back to the iconoclasm of the Reformation, but it is rooted also in the American sense of being in a new country, free from the wearying and repetitive ties of the Old World. To perpetuate Old World rituals, in Christmas cakes or christening dresses or holiday giving, in marriage ceremonies or mourning rites, has meant in the United States a kind of clinging to an ethnic past; these rituals suggest a failure to become fully American. Only those ceremonies distinctively American—in contrast to European, or in more recent years, Japanese and Middle Eastern—have been accepted fully and happily in the United States. But here again we have had difficulties; the ever-present new arrival in this country—new immigrant or critical visitor—has rejected the purely American ceremonials as no ceremonials at all. Americans in turn who have accepted this devaluation have been heard to comment: "We don't have anything but turkeys on Thanksgiving, while Europe has all those beautiful old ceremonies and customs."

Any child can delight in any ritual occasion, filled with color and food and the delightful reassurance of repetition combined with a chance for some innovation: "I'll make the place cards this year; you can make the turkeys of cellophane." Thus children in the United States have continued to love these ceremonies that their parents believe they ought to despise. And so these events and their preparation are left to elementary school teachers and gift-card companies and the makers of party favors to exploit. Where we could learn about the joys of combining ritual with freshness—with the new baby or the new bride, the new movie camera or the new tape recorder—we learn extremely little because of these ingrained attitudes that somehow American ceremonial occasions, both religious and secular, are "boring" and "commercial."

Every 210 days in Bali occurs the feast of Galungan. Traveling theatrical companies, under religious auspices, go from village to village. Children shout for joy to see them coming, and no one complains that it is commercial for pig merchants to accompany the performers, busily selling the pigs needed for the Galungan feasts. But with our American contempt for, and neglect of, the delights of ceremony, we leave most of the decorations, the masks, the costumes, the table settings, the special food and flowers to commercial hands; then we complain that our holidays are commercialized.

Besides this repudiation of our distinctive styles of celebrating holidays and occasions, we Americans believe that *ritual* is a bad word. Bedtime rituals are the special attribute of neurotics; bureaucratic rituals are the mark of large organizations that enslave the mind. *Ritualistic* means empty, formal, soulless, when applied as an adjective. And our odd definition of ritual as bad prompts an intolerance of all repetition. We don't want to read the same book twice or to see the same play over again or to be betrayed into viewing again the same program on television.

Every year I send my students to observe and to try to understand some religious service that is totally strange to them. A few years ago, a student elected to study a Roman Catholic mass. At first, delighted with the unfamiliar splendor of form and color and with the involvement of the senses, she worked along happily, observing and appreciating; then she reported, "Suddenly I realized: they do this *every* Sunday." Her powers of observation were paralyzed by this discovery. It had never occurred to her that any group of people would even do anything twice, to say nothing of every day, or every Sunday in the year, year after year.

In the 1970's young people have been demanding more life and color, more contemporaneousness in their lives; they have responded to this depreciation of existing ceremonial and to the belief that ritual is bad by trying to invent absolutely new things —"happenings"—with form and content completely unpredictable and new. But each of these inventions has become stylized, stereotyped, repetitive, and boring to those who perform and those who watch. The shallowness of a tradition of complete improvisation and absolute lack of predictability lacks the essential elements of great celebrations in which tried forms, polished by years of loving use, are infused with new life, ritualistic events which can be enjoyed just because the forms themselves or the content are familiar.

One ability that man lacks—at least as far as he has now evolved—is the ability to invent continually something entirely new. Real innovation is rare and inexpressibly precious, set as it always is within a rich and productive legacy from the past, or a shared view of the present or the future. And if the greatly original artist has to create the kind of tradition on which other artists are able to draw, too much energy goes into creating such forms. Endless (and inevitably mediocre) innovation is far more stereotyped than traditional form; we end up not with miracle plays or Verdi or Gilbert and Sullivan but with the themes of grade B movies and soap operas. One mediocrity cannot be distinguished from another, as each insists on being different with a genre too feeble to nourish any real originality.

A major function of ritual in human society is to permit those who are appropriately gifted to work together on forms that will be available to everyone, including those who are religiously gifted but who lack the power to express their experience in forms that are available to others.

A good ritual is very much like a natural language. The important thing about a natural language (in contrast to a technical language created for some special purpose) is that it has been spoken for a very long time by very many kinds of people—geniuses and dullards, old people on the verge of dying and children just learning to speak, men and women, good people and bad people, farmers and scholars and fishermen. It has become a language that everyone can speak and everyone can learn, a language that carries overtones of very old meanings and the possibilities of new meanings. I think we can describe ritual in exactly the same way. It must be old, otherwise it is not polished. It must be old, otherwise it cannot reflect the play of many men's imaginations. It must be old, otherwise it will not be fully available to everyone born within that tradition. Yet it also must be alive and fresh, open to new vision and changed vision.

The essence of ritual is the ability of the known form to reinvoke past emotion, to bind the individual to his own past experience, and to bring the members of the group together in a shared experience. "We Shall Overcome" is not only a moving song of hope, but it carries with it, when sung again, memories like the August, 1963, March on Washington, participated in life or on television by hundreds of thousands all over the United States; it lives and is sung within a tradition of shared musical style.

Celebrations answer the needs of each age: of the youngest child—first enthralled by the lights of candles on a cake or electrically lighted trees; of the older child beginning to remember and to forget his early childhood; of the adolescent hovering between a past that he must leave and a future that is not yet; of young parents, partly caught by memories of their parents; of grandmothers living again in the so different eyes of their grandchildren; of great-grandparents, living longer than people have ever lived and trying hard to learn how to remain in touch with the modern world. A celebration must be a ceremony in which each finds something together. It must be a community ceremonial if it is to have a place for each of them. One imaginative young bride and groom recently planned as the music for their wedding favorite dance tunes from the last five decades; thus each generation relived its youth, but all within the same framework, around the traditional marriage service, and with new and unfamiliar music for the present.

There are many ways in which communities—communities of all ages, or of many different ethnic and racial backgrounds —in religious and in secular ceremonial can celebrate with enough of past ritual to give shape and form to their feeling and to bind them together, and with enough that is new to make them feel alive and newly related to God, to all creation, to their fellowmen, to men long since dead, and to children yet to be born. Men, as biological creatures, share many needs with other primates and with living creatures even farther removed from them—with birds, with fish, even with plants. But human beings also have distinctive needs of their own: to relate to the supernatural, to the universe, and to each other—not through the simple immediacies of sight and hearing, touch and taste and smell, but through the complex and evocative ceremonial which men through the ages have developed to dance, to sing, to mime, and to dramatize these relationships. If we are to have real celebrations that do not pall or peter out because of the shallowness of their inspiration, we must have an informed and excited mix of the ceremonial inventions of other ages and other people. Only thus can the new sparkle like a jewel—in a setting which, because it is familiar, sets it off.

Two dangers are inherent in ritual. One is when the ritual is too rich and the highly elaborated symbolism too old to be appropriate to contemporary life. When this happens, one finds people who are overwhelmed, detached, alienated, and apathetic. Then again, where the individual's imagination, or the imagination of a whole group, is capable of expression that is denied by the poverty of a symbolic system, one may find glossolalia—speaking in tongues, abandoning the structure of conventional speech—and states of mind that resemble schizophrenia. In fact, where the individual has no way of setting his vision, his hope, or his need within any kind of boundaries, within the framework of any formal symbolic presentation, one is likely to find the most varied forms of aberrant behavior. Perhaps these two dangers, existing side by side in our contemporary American life, have prompted those strange doings and forms of expressions attributed to the hippie movement. These flower children cannot identify with the older forms and their own imaginations cannot adequately provide acceptable new forms, not even in drug-induced hallucinations.

Today's young people are attempting to exploit the senses directly, without the mediation of crystallized past delights. Partly this is because we as a people have been so grudging in our own contribution to the arts that delight, and partly because the young do not yet realize that there is nothing new that can be fully human unless it is partly contained within previous forms. This enormously alive modern period with access to the drama, the ritual, the beauty of celebrations all over the world provides us with unprecedented opportunities to draw upon. But it will take the combined efforts of mature artists, dramatists, choreographers, poets, together with the vivid young, to take advantages of this treasure house.

Culture is built by *all* the participants; when it is the creation of only one age group (as traditional American culture and modern Israeli culture have been the creation of young immigrant adults), everyone suffers. The present movement toward more emphasis upon joy can be seen as a new attempt to make our culture whole. Youth is clamoring and dancing; the adults have to supply part of the script or youth will itself be deprived of its heritage.

XIII Cultural Contexts of Aging
(1970)

Every human culture makes provision for the biological aspects of human growth and maturation, so that children are cared for during their long dependency, men and women of reproductive age are able to reproduce and care for the young, and those beyond reproductive age are given culturally regular ways of living out their old age. In very primitive cultures many human infants have to be sacrificed to the rigors of life, and the aged who are unable to play an active role may also have to be sacrificed. But during the long centuries since man became sedentary, and dependent upon agriculture rather than hunting and fishing, human cultures have developed a variety of ways in which the later years of life were stylized and given significance.

In addition to ways of life which simply ensured nurture, survival, and care for each age group, cultures have varied in the importance they assigned to different ages, sometimes giving more weight to childhood, sometimes to maturity, sometimes to old age. Those cultures which have valued wisdom and experience have found a readier way of dignifying age than have those cultures in which physical strength, warlike prowess, or physical or mental adventurousness are at a premium. The extent to which cultural phrasing of the importance of aging can overcome the actual physical setting of life is especially attested to in Australia, aboriginal cultures, where a nomadic people dependent upon hunting and food-gathering under conditions of extreme difficulty nevertheless accorded high respect to the old men.

American society today is attempting consciously to alter attitudes and practices in respect to the third quarter century of life, under the recognition of a number of changed conditions: increasing urbanization which makes for smaller houses and a lesser role for the aged; the increasing life-span of our population; and a greater sensitivity to the needs of each human being within our society. Any alteration of attitudes will have to take place within the framework of American culture, and this chapter is devoted to a brief enumeration of some aspects of American culture which are particularly relevant.

American culture values autonomy. We begin to teach children autonomy almost as soon as they are born, we reward children as they attain autonomy, and we regard the loss of autonomy as personally humilitating and socially lamentable. Any change in the attitude toward the elderly must take this into account. It will be more practical to ask: How can the elderly maintain autonomy? than: How can we make Americans accept a loss of autonomy in themselves or others?

In order to preserve the autonomy of the elderly so that they may respect themselves and receive respect from others, we need to develop not only financial provisions which make independence possible, but also the type of physical setting within which older people can live with dignity. This means types of housing adapted to age, no steps, simple housekeeping devices, availability of visiting nurse and cooked food services, and easy access to the society of other people of different ages. One of the potent factors in the lack of self-respect of, and respect for, the elderly is a deteriorated standard of living which is partly financial and partly due to living conditions which are too exacting and unsuitable.

American culture values upward gradients. We ask how fast a baby is growing, how much a school child is improving, how a man is "going up in the world." We give rewards not so much for achievement as for increasing achievement, we value the distance "from log cabin to White House" because it represents a long upward gradient. As American society is organized at present it is only possible in a few unique cases—academic and political figures who become the recipients of a series of awards and honors in their old age—for men and women to continue to achieve greater and greater successes right up to the end of their lives. As soon as individuals retire, or even reach a stable position from which further advancement is unlikely, their prestige tends to decline. This tendency to recognize only continuous immediate success, and to ignore past successes or high status which is unlikely to be capped by higher status, could be met, in the case of attitudes toward the aging, by cultural provisions for men and women of fifty or sixty to begin entirely new activities within which they might again rise.

It should be possible within the context of American culture for the initial shift to be downward, if the shift is accompanied by the idea of a "new start." Traditionally we have admired the man who "began all over again" in a new place, or after a severe financial setback, and this admiration could be channeled so that the man or woman who, in late middle age, voluntarily gave up a secure position to "start over" would initially be given support and approval. If this new start were in some field in which steady, although perhaps unspectacular progress were possible, and in which the preservation of a high standard of performance *in spite of* failing faculties could be dramatized, such shifts might provide part of the solution.

American culture is oriented toward the two-generation family, consisting of parents and minor children. Within this pattern there is slight place for grandparents. This problem is being partially met by the institution of the "sitter" under which guise grandparents again re-enter the homes of their married children. Further recognition of the value of grandparents in stabilizing children's personality by giving them a coherent picture of what their own later years may in part be like, should also help to restore the role of grandparents. But it must be recognized that in a rapidly changing culture, young parents who do not themselves know what the future will bring are likely to remain the most appropriate mentors of the young and that the grandparents' role in such a culture is likely to remain supplementary.

American culture to an increasing extent focuses marriage around the shared upbringing of children rather than around the other activities such as shared production, shared money-making, etc. which have given husbands and wives common interests in other cultures. This emphasis results in couples whose children have been reared facing a period of life in which they have no vivid shared activity. There are various ways in which this problem might be met: a second set of children born late in life after a first set have grown up and left home is one solution which may postpone the age at which the parents are left alone from forty to sixty. If the idea of a shift in occupation in late middle age were to become general, this might also involve a shift in residence and living habits which could be used as a basis for the development of a new common interest in the life of the pair.

American culture is oriented toward the values associated with youth, spontaneity, physical vigor, impulse fulfillment in simple direct terms, combined with a youthful appearance and manner. These values allow scant place for age except for those who by some miracle manage to look or act as much younger than they are. In this particular period of history, changes in styles, cosmetics, and plastic surgery have made it possible for almost every woman to "look younger than she is," which gives a temporary respite to an aging woman, but cannot be relied upon for the future, as the children growing up today will have learned to see the woman who looks "young" to her near contemporaries as "old." Only a genuine change in cultural emphasis from the values of sheer spontaneity and freshness to values associated with experience, connoisseurship, and increasing taste and wisdom are likely to stem this particular trend.

In American culture each individual life is regarded as a unique event, having a beginning and an end (in contrast to those cultures which believe in reincarnation), and there is a related emphasis on the ease of learning at the beginning and the difficulty of learning at the end. There is some evidence to suggest that the way in which older people are able to learn is related to the way in which children originally learn to learn. For example, an individual who has learned that foreign languages are easy and natural to learn, and has mastered two or more languages in early childhood, will find it less difficult to learn a new language at fifty than will someone who learned as a child that it was "not natural" to speak any language except English. It is quite possible that we will be able to change our methods of teaching children so as to make it possible for older people to learn new skills with the facility which they show in cultures like Bali, where the end of life is regarded as the end of one reincarnation, and people master new skills very late in life, with ease and success.

American culture lays great stress on "being loved," "being wanted," and a corresponding stress on the obligations to arouse and to supply these feelings. This stress, in the case of people with grown children, conflicts with the American premium on young people living by themselves and upon parents "not interfering." It is suggested that we might consciously develop ways in which older people become essential and important in the lives of younger people not their own children. Such an adjustment might be encouraged in a number of ways, such as the development of a style of behavior which would call for people changing their doctors and lawyers at fifty, and choosing younger practitioners; such a procedure would cement ties between older patients and younger practitioners and therefore between younger patients and older practitioners and become one two-way process by which more intermeshing of the lives of old and young—outside the immediate family— might be accomplished.

One of the overall difficulties of readjusting our attitudes toward old age comes from the often expressed belief that in the past old people used to be more stalwart; that all of the grandparents of the present grandparents lived to a ripe old age and hardly needed glasses at eighty. This belief is partly an idealization of the past and partly due to the type of selectivity in an earlier age which permitted only the very hardy to survive. The larger number of elderly people who are kept alive by modern medicine fosters an underlying sense of bitterness and complaint in the middle-aged of today, who feel they are unduly burdened by parents who have lost a socially significant role, and who detract from their abilities to provide for their children who represent the future.

In such a situation it is all the more pressing to have a new cultural orientation toward the place of the elderly, who must be given a significant place in our society if that society is to have full humanity. We are moving toward a definition of the good society as one in which every age is valued for itself and asked to contribute as itself, rather than valued as a prelude or honored as a postlude to activities at some other age.

Aging Different in the Space Age

I think the attitude in the United States, that old age is a form of illness to be lamented but not mentioned earlier than necessary, has been part of our whole cult of youth and our unwillingness to tackle head-on many of the aspects of aging, especially, of course, that it will ultimately end in death—an idea which we've been extraordinarily unwilling to face or to discuss.

When I went back to the Manus Islands in the Pacific in 1953 to deal with the people who had skipped over two thousand years and come directly into the modern world, I found that they had learned to record age and time perfectly, beginning with 1946. Before 1946, things were a total blank. After 1946, they recorded birth dates down to the hour of birth. The village clock wasn't always right, but at least it recorded some time that could be put on the birth record. And with the greatest, most meticulous care, they were recording every single date from 1946 on.

I asked them, "How do you know that this year is 1953?"

They said, "Well, last year was 1952. True? And the year before that and the year before that and then there was 1946 —that's when our life began."

And I said, "How do you know what year that was?"

And they said, "Because the Europeans told us so."

And they were hanging suspended in this narrow little piece of time and they thought that all of us could name all our ancestors back to Adam—with middle names—and that they alone of the peoples of the world had been so deprived that they didn't know the names of their great-great-great-great-great-grandfathers. They didn't think it was very far back to Adam either—just a few generations.

I decided to make three charts in order to place them correctly in time. One, geological time, showed how late man appeared on the scene. The second chart showed the dates that were significant to them as a people and their way of looking at the world—the birth of Jesus, the discovery of America, the discovery of Australia, the discovery of New Guinea, World War I, World War II, and 1946—which were the only dates that mattered to them.

And third, because I had been in the village twenty-five years before and could make a pretty good guess, I made a time scale, by decades of birth dates on which the living people had been born. They could then fit themselves into the biology of the present and begin to think of fifty and sixty years ago, in terms of the ages of people who were right around them.

This was a very simple form of orientation. It's one we sometimes neglect because we still take children to school and have them write on the board, "September 3, 1954." And the child asks, "What's that?" And the teacher says, "It's the date." Whether they know what a date is or not doesn't matter. Sometimes they don't find out what "B.C." means for years.

Now, we have a much more complicated thing to do and we don't always do it very completely. We not only have to trace our maturing and aging population in time, with our knowledge of the development of man and our knowledge of our own history, and our knowledge of how old everybody is around us, but we also have to have a model that moves. The picture of aging that people of my day grew up with is no longer valid and the aging that our children will do is totally different from the aging that we have today.

One of the complications, of course, is how to handle this moving model of aging and not pickle or crystallize it in our institutions, whether they be social security regulations, residence laws, rules for the construction of buildings or about driving cars, or any of the thousands of ways in which aging is engaged with the structure of society.

We have to be very careful that we don't do anything with the group that we are dealing with now that might limit the possibilities of people who will be the same age twenty years from now. This has been one of our big drawbacks in any kind of social research in this country.

We catch a group of adolescents and we make a study about their childhood and we find out what their mothers did that they shouldn't have done and what they didn't do that they should have done. Then we go back and try to change what's happening to today's babies, so that future adolescents won't be like the adolescents we've got now. We don't allow for the fact that today's babies are being brought up differently anyway, and so we're always trying to catch up with ourselves. We have to take into account how we're going to see the difference between the decades in our history. We must not let the special characteristics of the people who were born in 1890 determine what we're going to do for people who were born in 1920. We must be ever mindful that in building a moving model of aging, we must build in ways to allow for all these differences.

There must be provision made for the difference, for instance, between older people who enjoy television and those who do not. An eighty-year-old retired factory worker who never went to the movies might not be amused by television. He might not see anything entertaining on the screen at all. However, the person who forty years from now will be eighty might have a consummate belief that there is a great deal on the screen. All we'll need to do for these people is install a television screen to keep them perfectly quiet; we won't need tranquilizers anymore.

There is obviously a tremendous difference between people who grew up before there was so much noise and the people who grow up today, who weave a cocoon of their own noise around themselves and thereby seem to protect themselves from everybody else's noise. If you have your own television going full tilt and an air conditioner, you don't hear other people's televisions and other people's air conditioners; you just hear the roar. People of today are better attuned to roars and are less likely to choose quiet than people of the past would be.

There are very large numbers of these variants, so many that twenty-five years ago even to mention them would in a sense have been very disturbing and depressing. They would have said, and with fair justice: We can't take all of these things into account. We can't look at all of the differences in the life-span of individuals, and where they were born and where their parents were born and what their religion is, was, and is going to be; and what their parents were and weren't and all of their occupations and their order of birth and all their living experiences, in small towns or in big cities or in intimate slums or in unintimate housing projects. We can't deal with all of this. There are too many variables; we'll just have to settle down. Over sixty-five, we know who they are; they are aging.

This is the policy that was put into effect in many places. A psychiatric study was made in England wherein a large group of people were diagnosed as senile dementia, and therefore, a certain number of years later all ought to have been dead. They looked at the ones who weren't dead and they found they hadn't had senile dementia at all; they were just sixty-five years of age and over and had had other things wrong with them.

But it was very hard to deal with anything broader. It was very discouraging for social scientists to come along and say all of these things made a difference.

Today this isn't so. You can program any number of variables into a little computer. You can really dsicriminate between different kinds of people and discriminate with enough style and care so that we don't have to lump people anymore. Fairly soon we'll be able to have physiological measures of aging that will give us something like "retirement readiness," just as we have for small children what we call "reading readiness."

Quite clearly then, from such a physiological measure we should be able, quite soon, to discriminate among groups of people in terms of their readiness to retire, their need to retire, and the need of the organization they work in to be freed of their presence, which is considerable in many instances—especially, I imagine, those offices that are covered by our Civil Service regulations, which do beget a kind of peacefulness, shall we say, in the older echelons.

Hopefully, we'll be able to look at a lot of these things differently than we do now. We'll be able to recognize that to talk about somebody at a given age, without considering his generational position, isn't very sensible.

Now, I had a very prolonged, argumentative conversation with a specialist in the field who was telling me what grandmothers wanted. After I listened for an hour about these grandmothers, I demanded that we stop and consider: Was this man talking about grandmothers or great-grandmothers? In fact, he actually was talking about groups of people all of whom could have been great-grandmothers, and many of whom were.

I submit that a grandmother and a great-grandmother are quite different. Any woman who has first brought up her own children and then brought up a whole batch of grandchildren deserves to be tired when she's a great-grandmother. And she's legitimately tired. It's only the really energetic that want to bring up great-grandchildren.

But the grandmother who has her first grandchild at sixty is a very different person from the great-grandmother who is seventy.

The man who just trailed along and didn't amount to much until he was about forty-five, and then bloomed, has a very different attitude toward life at sixty-five than a boy who went to work at fourteen.

We've got to stop thinking about a category of grandmothers who all look like what we think our grandmothers looked like —if we can remember them. Of course, they looked terribly old —incredibly old—as older people always look to children. Then we've had this continuous process of rejuvenation going on in my lifetime. All the women in my age group, and slightly above it, benefit by the fact that they look younger every year.

We need to think in terms of generational, as well as chronological age—definitely and precisely. We must not lump together and confuse sixty-five to seventy-five years of age, for instance, with being grandparents or great-grandparents. Some are, some never were, and some never will be. Don't mix the spinster with the woman who has borne many children. Don't mix either one with the woman who has been married and never had children. Don't mix the man who is just hitting his stride and the man who is a master of a particular skill that is disappearing and treat them in the same way.

Again, this is something everybody knows. But I don't think we can emphasize strongly enough that although we know it, we're not doing enough with it. We're going right along talking about these poor old grandmothers who want to be disengaged from life and so we do housing studies and we ask them, "Would you rather live in a noisy neighborhood, filled the other people's children and dogs, or would you rather live in a nice, peaceful, quiet place built for old people like yourself?"

The answer is they say they'd rather live in a nice, peaceful, quiet place. Nobody finds out how many dogs and children they've had in their lives all along nor what the older person's image of this nice, peaceful, quiet place—these ghettos that we're building for older people—is. Many of them are being built in California now. Nobody under fifty is allowed; it's a kind of reverse maternity ward.

Nowadays there are also a number of people who have gone through two generations of life, and in many cases also nursed their aging mothers and their aging fathers, and who would like to retire quietly and think or pray or live with their sisters—all of these various forms of disengagement from contemporary life.

By stylizing older people as grandparents we muddle it all up and we don't use the grandparents as we should. We're not recognizing that grandparents are, on the whole, the most vigorous, freest group in the population. Many of the men have gone as far as they are going to get, so they can stop competing. If they are women, they are filled with mild postmenopausal zest.

We should be using them in the community. They should never get categorized in any way as retired, as out of the picture. We should have grandparents and teachers' associations, or grandparents' and school associations.

Today we retire people from community life the day their last child leaves public school. They may be only forty, but we put them on the shelf. They turn into disgruntled taxpayers who disapprove of the schools and object to the bond issue.

Every community in the country is filled with these people and it's utterly unnecessary. We should recognize that they are still young and shouldn't be put into this category. The fact that they are grandparents does not put them into an aging category at all. Aging is for great-grandparents and great-great-grandparents. I can say this with a certain amount of conviction because I could be a great-grandparent this moment. My great-grandchild would be my daughter's daughter's child, probably, and not a son's son's child. But still, I could be a great-grandparent this minute, and it highlights the way we've been mixing generations, and relations to children, and relations to society, and chronological age, and confusing the general picture that we are working on.

When we use the words "the golden years of life," roughly speaking, we are thinking of the great-grandparents, and great-great-grandparents. Up to that point, we call them "silver." This "golden" business, of course, I don't think we are going to give up quite yet, though I imagine there are going to be a fairly large number of people who are going to rebel against being "golden" and I think it might be a good idea if they did.

In the same way that we have to figure all these generational differences, we also have to figure the kind of medical care that people have had, and this is going to be a tremendously important factor—say for the next twenty or thirty years. After that, hopefully, we will not have citizens who will suffer the kind of neglect that our aging citizens have suffered in the past. We won't have the same kind of medical problems and older people won't present the same kind of picture to young people that they present today.

This is, I think, one of the very important points to worry about. My generation and the generations immediately above mine, grew up with a mandate from society to live under all circumstances: Times were going to be tough. Getting through your second summer was something many babies didn't do, and the ones that managed to live through their second summer had to go through all the diseases of the period. We had to live through diphtheria and scarlet fever and typhoid and pneumonia and gain weight, and then we were good babies. When you build this much goodness and will to live into a young child, it lasts into old age. Today it lasts into an old age that's totally different from the old age that I saw as a child.

I was figuring it out the other day. I was twenty-six or twenty-seven before I saw an old human vegetable. This is serious. In other words, all the old people I knew were people one wanted to emulate; they were lively. They tatted without their glasses. They could still read fine print. Their minds were alert. They were a little deaf and they had a lot of rheumatism, but nevertheless, they were lively, interesting people. The picture of aging, therefore, combined with "you must live through diphtheria, measles, whooping cough, scarlet fever, pneumonia, and someday, if you're good, you'll be old"—this was a very rewarding picture.

The young people who are growing up today are seeing the

consequences of this attitude. They are seeing people who will hang on to life against their own wishes as they are kept alive by our modern methods of medical care—methods they couldn't have dreamed of in their childhood. In this way they have no opportunity to form a determination "not to age." But the new generation will have this opportunity. A new generation will have a different attitude toward human dignity and will be able to set their sights quite differently.

We have to be continually aware of those people who grew up in and outlived one age and are growing old and dying in another, so that they will not set a standard or depress the expectations of younger people, but rather, that they will be able to communicate to younger people other sorts of things.

We must demonstrate why this group of aged people need this kind of care—because they had no education, because they are illiterate, because they moved from one country to another and never learned the new language, because they lived in the slums, because they had no medical care, because they had bad nutrition, because their image of themselves was built in an earlier period. The people today who are grandparents and are moving into a later period with a fuller realization of what aging means—far better medical care and nutrition—are going to be different kinds of people.

When I read that Winston Churchill was retiring, I was reminded of an old woman of ninety in Devon, England, during World War II. She was one of the people who tatted without her glasses. My aunt had given her money for some tatting that the old woman had made for her, and the old woman said it was too much.

"You paid me too much. You paid me more than it's worth and I won't take it."

And my aunt said, "Never mind, Mary! Give it to a good cause."

So the old woman thought for a moment and said, "Well, that

little old man with a cigar in his mouth, he'll be retiring some-day and we'll need a present for him."

In building a program for this kind of change we must keep out of the future the deficiencies of the present, and recognize that what we're doing now is merely palliative. It's making up for the mistakes of the past; it's making up for the changes of the past; it's making up for people who were undernourished in their childhood and whose aging process shows it. At the same time, we are designing for the next twenty, thirty, or forty years a completely different kind of relationship to older people who will be alertly related to the young people and to the community.

This is a difficult thing to do. There will be a great many borderline cases. I suppose we'll have to have a computer to cope with them, too. But it is possible if we start with a community organization that will use grandparents much more than they do now. This will prepare the way for a different kind of participation by the older people. It isn't enough just to have 10 percent of public housing set up for old people. We need more intricate relationships.

We could start, for instance, by eliminating "Den Mothers." Den mothers are one of the nuisances that have been invented in this world. They are bad for little boys and they are bad for the mothers. They just perpetuate too much female society mixed up with learning how to be a man.

There are unlimited potential candidates for "Den Grandfathers" around and they are at least as able to do the things den mothers do—and a whole lot of other things that den mothers can't do. So, if we could set up grandparents and teachers' associations, and get the grandparents back in the schools; if we could set up den grandfathers instead of den mothers; if we could do things such as are being planned now by the Oliver Wendell Holmes Association, we might make some progress. The Oliver Wendell Holmes Association is planned for the affluent, but nevertheless can have repercussions in models that we can use at every level. The Association offers courses of high academic excellence to people's parents and parents-in-law while they're on vacation so that when they go back home after four months in Florida, they'll be very up to date.

In fact, they'll be more up to date than their children because they'll have time to learn something. It will be possible to feed back into the communities remarkably well-informed older people with time to read the newspapers, and time to read Plato, and time to keep alive a knowledge of our tradition. But at the same time, this will be related to the present, and so they can teach their grandchildren and their great-grandchildren what they know far better than any young person: the nature of change itself.

We have been so impressed in this country with putting grandparents on the shelf because they came from some other country, and they didn't get on with the visiting nurse. The general style of the row between the grandmother and the visiting nurse, plus the row between the two sets of parents-in-law, has become crystallized in the way we handle things. We have assumed that on the whole, grandparents and old people are a liability. Old people that talk only about the past are just as tiresome as people who talk only about the present. But old people who can describe vividly and meaningfully to young people the steps from candles to kerosene lamps, to gas lamps, to electricity; who can describe the steps from nothing but the newspaper and the telegraph to the Morse code, to radio and television, and then Telestar—these people have an invaluable contribution to make in building into our young people a notion of flexibility—a recognition that the world twenty years from now is going to be incredibly different from the world of the present day.

The only people who really know that fact with absolute conviction are older people. They know that the past was different, even though young people think that the world was always "transistorized." The young never lived in any other kind of world. They cannot imagine another kind of world, unless they are given help. They become so rigidly committed to orange juice and interior plumbing that they are unable to move around. A lot of preparatory work has been done in the Peace Corps. It's done very well, generally, and our young people learn that people eat other foods, speak other languages, and live in other kinds of houses. But even with the very dedicated group in the Peace Corps, it takes time to teach them.

And we've found in the past that when we compared primitive people where grandparents were important, and primitive people where they weren't, that the grandparents made for conservatism, while the societies in which children were brought up by parents and didn't know yet about the end of life, these societies were more progressive and more flexible. But this was in a society that was almost static.

In a relatively static society, too much association with grandparents makes one static, but in a changing and moving society, the only certain way that one can keep a sense of change and movement is to associate with grandfather and let him talk about the past, and fill the listening children's ears with the idea that the world has changed incredibly.

The world has changed, is changing, and will change, and those who have changed most are the older people. They are the best living example of change.

All this is going to require a tremendous amount of imagination in the way we structure the relationship of older people to the community. We will have to sort out those who are ready for retirement at an early age because of the vicissitudes of their lives and who need only protection and cherishing and care. We can't do very much more for them now, because in the past we weren't able to do very much or didn't try to. Yet, we must do this without building a picture of aging in the future that is going to include any of these things. Instead, we must develop a picture for the future in which we will have the sort of community, the sort of housing, the sort of educational assistance in which people never finish school, in which we never put husky sixty-five-year-old people into ghettos, and in which we are able to use almost all the grandparent generation and many of the great-grandparent generation in building a society that is flexible enough to be continually self-renewing—continually able to change.

XIV The Right To Die
(1968)

Human beings have no control over their births. They cannot choose to whom they will be born, when, or where, or who their brothers and sisters will be. Each of us is faced, as consciousness dawns, with a set of irrevocable circumstances which determine to a very great extent what our lives will be. Although there have been peoples who believed otherwise, for example the Omaha Indians, who believed that twin children had chosen their parents, there seems no chance that this helpless relationship to one's biological beginnings will be altered. We then proceed to work out as much freedom and autonomy for each individual as the current state of this social system will allow. In the United States we have gone a long way toward such autonomy. Whom one will marry, whether or not to have children, what job to take, where to live, are matters that are free from the veto of relatives and that we are trying to free from economic constraints also. And almost every baby born today will reach adulthood.

But our new medical knowledge and skills have curtailed one freedom that our ancestors were able to express more fully than we now can. In the past there were no methods for keeping alive people long after their brains had ceased to give them any conscious relation to the world around them. One could approach old age with the expectation of death uncomplicated by the fear of living months, or even years, as an expensive human vegetable.

Today this possibility hangs over all Americans as they approach old age, bringing fear of being "kept alive" beyond any hope of ever again being humanly related to the family and friends who care for them.

Yet it is an essential part of our present medical progress that physicians and nurses are pledged to preserve life in every person, regardless of age or sex, race or status, as long as the last breath of life flickers within him. Without this pledge we would not have modern medical care. But with it we face this new problem of the stricken or the elderly who are preserved far beyond what they or those who love them would choose for them.

We cannot ask either physician or nurse for relief. They must remain absolutely pledged to life. But there is another recourse. If an individual is conscious, he may refuse an operation, or a blood transfusion, or any other medical remedy that is recommended. And just as it is possible to make a will, stating that one is of sound mind, many years before one's death, so it is possible to make a legal statement—while one is of sound mind—forbidding medical intervention which may result in states which, while called life, nevertheless mean a life without meaning, when one is only a burden to others. Just as a physician honors a patient's refusal of surgery, so such a duly executed statement can be honored. Once made, it means that the old can live out their lives without the haunting fear of witless dependency.

But this is still negative; it is the right not to be saved, rather than a positive right to choose the point where one's usefulness is ended. Long ago, among the Eskimos, who lived very close to starvation, an old person who could no longer contribute to the well-being of the family group could elect to die, with dignity. Today we do not judge the worth of an elderly person by his economic contribution; but we do still judge his contribution as a sentient human being. I believe that we can develop an ethic whereby individuals can not only guard against being kept alive—as, without an expression from them, they must be —but can also elect to die.

The present generation of old people cannot make that choice. The will to live which carried them through the hazards of childhoods is still so strong that they live on for years, unable to die. But they are also educating their descendants who, watching them live on, without meaning, can begin to form a quiet determination that they, themselves, will never continue to cling to a life after meaning has fled.

Today's middle-aged will be able to develop a new attitude toward their own lives, welcoming a longevity that keeps them human but consciously moving away from the inhuman longevity which they have witnessed and from which they have suffered.

The present interest in heart transplants is raising pertinent questions, with suggestion that the old criteria of life—a heartbeat and respiration—should be altered and that irreversible brain death should instead be substituted. If these criteria were to be accepted, then by society's redefinition, one of the nightmares which haunt the aging would be removed.

Euthanasia is a horrible idea. No society that can afford to care for its old can condemn them to death or grudge them care. Only by the acts of individuals, when they are still young enough and strong enough to make their own plans, can we hope to combine our high level of medical and nursing care and medical and nursing responsibility, our affluence which makes it impossible for us to refuse care, with our respect for individual integrity and the right to choose.

XV Ritual Expression
of the Cosmic Sense
(1966)

Is it possible to work out a formulation—of the kind anthropologists try for when we are studying a culture—that would describe the liturgical movement? The problem, it seems to me, is how to bring together within one context the desire to break down all barriers—the barriers separating bishops and other people, those separating the races of men, and those separating the laity (although one hears about lay men and lay women, nothing is said about lay children; I presume that sooner or later they will be included)—the desire to go back into the past and push forward into the future, and the desire to include the disreputable. In another period we would have said "the humble and lowly;" today, I think "disreputable" is one aspect of the more inclusive attempt to reach out to all those whose feet have been unwashed through the ages (and whenever the feet of some new group are washed, this shocks some people); it is part of the attempt to include all those who are denigrated and lost, as well as the dispossessed of our slums, urban and rural, and, beyond our own country, all the peoples of the earth.

At this moment in history the desire to reach out toward all

men is entirely consistent with our new exploration, with the
efforts we are making to probe the depths of the sea, to move
out into outer space, and to consider whether the inhabitants
of earth (one no longer says "this earth" or "the earth" but just
"earth") are the only sentient creatures in the universe. From
an agelong concentration on our world we are moving out to
include the solar system, the galaxy, and we do not yet know
how far beyond.

One other thing should also be included in the context of
what we desire to bring together in a new whole. This is the
beauty of liturgy. The use of precious metals, beautiful fabrics,
and rich colors are all part of this. I think it is important to bear
this in mind, for while we may feel it is wrong to spend money
on precious vestments as long as there are hungry people, our
attempt to respond to hunger and poverty should not bar out
the development of every kind of beauty in the liturgy.

And now, if I were to describe the liturgical movement, I
would say that it is an extraordinary breaking of bounds—a
breaking of the boundaries that people feel have separated one
part of our lives from another part. As the eucharist is carried
into the simplest home, that home is broadened into a cathe-
dral; and at the same time, behavior within cathedrals seems to
be moving back and forth in an utterly unpredictable way.
Ritual is an exceedingly important part of all culture, all the
cultures we now know about and, hopefully, all the cultures we
shall know about in the future.

I could, of course, discuss the way fire and water, darkness
and light, earth and living things, are used the world over as
symbols of new life. I could describe the many forms of ritual
that break or purify man's tie to the earthly part of his nature,
all those beliefs and acts that bind together rituals in every part
of the world and create a resonance between the rituals of
Christianity and the rituals of other peoples and other religions.
Instead, I prefer to discuss what we know as scientists, as an-

thropologists, who study the different kinds of men inhabiting the earth and who now know that all men belong to one species. This is a biological affirmation of the idea of the Brotherhood of Man which the Church has always stood for but which many of its clergy and their congregations have found—and sometimes still find—difficult. But we now have a scientific basis for our belief in the brotherhood of man, something that is very helpful to modern clergy. We know that the tiniest Pygmy and the most isolated Australian aborigine are members of the same species to which we belong, and we know that all men share the same human characteristics as well as the characteristics that bind all of us equally to the rest of the natural world.

In the latter part of the nineteenth century and the beginning of the twentieth century scientists were fascinated, perhaps even obsessed, with the problem of how man is like the primates, the birds, and other living creatures; their studies emphasized what has so felicitously been called our creatureliness. But scientists working in the second half of the twentieth century have begun, and I think will continue, to explore those things that are unique to man. For although we eat and drink and sleep and care for our young as many other living creatures do, man also has certain characteristics, identifiable by ordinary scientific methods of research, that are unique to his species.

One of these peculiarly human characteristics is man's search for meaning in the universe. This search for meaning has been called the *cosmic sense* or, sometimes, the cosmological sense, but I prefer the simpler term. Slowly, as we have begun to identify many more than the traditional "five senses," we have also come to realize that there are many more ways in which man senses the universe. By the cosmic sense we mean man's need, a need found in every child and expressed in every culture, to relate to and understand the universe, so that individual life takes on meaning. Our knowledge of the cosmic sense comes, on the one hand, from the study of children and, on the other, from comparative studies of many different living cultures. On the basis of this knowledge it is possible to say that the need to find meaning in the universe is as real as the need for trust and for love, for relations with other human beings. It has been demonstrated that infants who are deprived of care by identifiable persons—infants in orphan asylums and foundling homes, who are well fed and medically cared for, but who have no single person to whom they can attach themselves—will die. It is a basic characteristic of human beings that, in infancy, they must have some close relationship to another human being in order to become human. So, equally, the need to have some relationship to the universe, to attach meaning to life, to perceive the outer world, to take it in and give something out, can be described as a basic human characteristic. And, of course, it is this need to which the whole liturgy of the Church gives particular expression.

In fact, speaking in tongues fits in exceedingly well with what I want to say. Think for a moment of the most expressive, gifted, and artistic person you have ever known, someone with the creative capacity to embody the deepest vision in a painting, in music, or in a ritual dance. Clearly, this creative ability is very rare and very imperfectly distributed among men. And now, for a moment, think of the deepest religious experience you have ever known, or, if you do not think your own religious experience has ever been equal to that of the saints, think about the deepest religious experience you have ever read about or encountered in another person. Clearly, the capacity for religious experience also is very imperfectly distributed among men. Moreover, these two capacities are very differently distributed among human beings. This was true even among the very simplest people I ever studied, a mountain people in New Guinea.

Only a very few people have the capacity for a transcendental experience of the world in depth and with strength. Now, if those with this capacity were also those who are gifted with creative capacities for expression in speech, in painting, or in immediate flowing prayer, we might perhaps not have the same need for ritual. For experience would immediately be matched by expression of that experience, and in some form it would be there to be shared by those who lack both the capacity for experience and the power of expression. But because they are differently distributed, we find an extreme contrast. At one end of the scale there are the elaborate, beautiful, formal rituals that have been worked on by aesthetically gifted individuals through the ages. And at the other end of the scale there are people, lacking any of these special gifts, whose religious experience breaks through all expression. I think the individual speaks in tongues when his capacity to give structure to experience breaks down, and at certain moments in history it happens that those who have strong, immediate feelings have no words, no acts, no symbols that will appropriately contain what they have experienced, and so they temporarily abandon the structure of speech.

Some societies, as a whole, are extraordinarily impoverished, in the sense that their ritual is very slight, their artistic forms are very slight, and, very often, their experience also is very thin. It is on ritual forms that the imagination of each generation feeds. Children have the need to seek for meaning in the world around them—in the natural world—and to seek for transcendence in that world. If the forms are there, polished through many generations by the imagination and gift of many people, children's imagination can be caught, invigorated, and illuminated by the forms that are there, ready for new expression. In a thin, poor, ritually impoverished environment this cannot happen.

Certain societies have elaborated to an extraordinary extent the human capacity for expression in music, art, and ritual. Bali is one of these. In Bali today, those who are concerned with the liturgical reform movement of the Roman Catholic Church are having a delightful time. The language has a resonance like the clanging of bells. The Balinese are so imaginative that they can produce a miracle play at a moment's notice. And they are such gifted carvers and painters that one has only to present them with a large blank wall and in no time at all they will produce the most magnificent gargoyles. The Balinese are, in fact, a people with an enormously informed imagination. For this reason, also, they are ready to take into their hands and their voices the outlines of the Christian tradition and to give Christian ritual a new and delightful form that reaches deep into their own symbolism.

In contrast, there are people who have almost no developed capacity for ritual expression. I have worked with a people whose major ritual act is to spit betel nut juice. The juice is rusty red. The betel nut itself is a beautiful bright green and has a spherical shape. The lime chewed with the nuts is white. If in a sermon one wants to make a spherical point, the shape of the betel nut can provide the necessary simile. But on the whole this is a meager assemblage, and the ceremony is a meager one to build on.

Comparing different cultures, the same cultures at different periods, and the several parts of a single tradition, we can find many contrasts of this kind. Within the Christian tradition we have had a lamentable tendency to go to extremes in separating out fragments of the whole. When such a fragmentation has occurred, those who have grasped at one fragment sometimes have thought of it not as a different expression of the whole, but instead as a rather willful version of the whole. Comparing many of these versions, we can see that there has been tremendous variation in the capacity of different groups to build rituals that are enduring and have the continuity necessary to make them available to all the people born within a society.

This is, as I understand it, what the liturgical movement is trying to do with the traditional ritual of the Church—to use the old symbols, but to use them with a lively, fresh insight that will free both the rituals and ourselves from the rigidity of forms that cannot contain new vision. This can happen to languages as well. We speak of a language as going through a period of great productivity and then sometimes as settling into a kind of rigidity that fossilizes and destroys the thought of a whole period.

Ritual must carry the continuity that makes a tradition available to all who live within it. But this is not its only function. Ritual also gives people access to intensity of feeling at times when responsiveness is muted. This is especially striking in the ceremonies of second mourning that occur in many parts of the world. Many peoples have such a ritual of second mourning, which usually serves to free the mourners from the obligatory observances of mourning. It may take place when the bones are dug up, when the head is taken and put somewhere else, when the widow or the parents are relieved of isolation, and so on. In different cultures any one of a whole series of acts may be the signal for the ceremony of second mourning. And then, at the critical time, the mourners are expected once more to mourn intensely. But as the ritual may take place a year or more after the bereavement, the mourners will no longer feel so desperately sad as they did when the death occurred. One of the peoples I studied in New Guinea have a way of jerking their heads to induce the feeling. On such an occasion the women sit and jerk their heads until at last they get into a state in which they can mourn as convincingly as on the day the person died. Their mourning has all the physiological qualities of the first expression of grief, and for the moment the original grief is reinstated and made vivid.

This, then, is a second function of ritual—to lift people above the dullness that inevitably follows on moments of high feeling and to reinstate the high ecstasy that is so transient an experience. The recurrence of the ritual assures them that the feeling once was there and may come back again. This is, of course, the principal function of the rituals of family relationships—wedding anniversaries, birthday celebrations, and family reunions —and of all those ceremonies where we attempt to reconstitute ritually a feeling that exists but that may lack any immediate power of expression. It is a second function of ritual all over the world.

At the present time, those who are working within the liturgical movement are seeking to produce an all-embracing form, a form that will gather into one whole all the peoples on earth, all the disciplines through which man learns, and all the places where we may go, and, in so doing, will illuminate the events of our time—the civil rights meetings, events taking place on the farthest island of the seas, and the celebration of Easter at the Holy Sepulchre in Palestine. Responding to the present, the liturgical movement can draw on our contemporary knowledge of human capacities and our recognition that the cosmic sense can be studied and understood and related to the rituals we shall build. And now at last the old argument between science and religion can be replaced by a dialogue in which all that we know scientifically from the study of man, especially from the study of children, will be illuminated by the historic and the contemporary inspiration of the Church.

XVI The Immortality of Man
(1957)

As the study of the cosmos has broadened man's sense of the universe in which he lives, the words of the Psalm:*

> The heavens declare the glory of God; and the firmament showeth his handiwork

have taken on very different meanings for the writer in 1600, 1800, and 1972. As the study of the fossils of the earth and of the changes in living forms have given new meaning to the condensed statements of creation of earlier times, so too we may expect the comparative study of the ways in which human beings have attempted to understand man as a being with a soul or spirit somehow separate from its corporeal abode to add new dimensions to our understanding of man's search for immortality. Each great religious system has carried within its explication the limitations imposed by the state of knowledge of its interpreters. While we may say that the very meaning of the word "prophet" is that his inspiration transcends the limitations of time and space and the state of man's knowledge within

*19:1.

which the prophecy is made, the inspiration must nevertheless be couched either in words of tremendous generality and universality or else in the homely figures of speech of those who listen, and then such a phrase as "in my Father's house are many mansions" loses its universality when the image is constructed with marble floors or tile roofs. Men will differ in their preferences for the bleak sweep of an infinity in which there is no familiar shape or color, or for some particular evocation which is within their narrow experience. Meanwhile, we may easily lose sight of the extent to which our present most lofty conceptions of man's place in the universe are limited and narrowed either by the provincialisms of Euro-American traditions or by the obstreperous materialism of a young scientific development.

Anthropological materials—that is, a comparative discussion based upon records of other, particularly of other more primitive, cultures—should be able to give us the means whereby we may assess the special character of our own historically limited approach to the question of immortality, and so deepen and widen our perception of the scope of the question. When Americans in 1972 think of immortality, they think of survival after death, of some other sphere or plane, and of the persistence of personal identity. And indeed at first glance it would seem quite difficult to think about immortality at all except in terms of these three ideas.

Yet each of these three—to us—essential aspects of immortality can be thought of, has been thought of, very differently. Let us take first the period of immortality, which we think of as beginning at birth, or at conception, and stretching onward forever. But there are people who are more concerned with pre-existence, as we would have to phrase it because of the importance which we attribute to this single existence on earth. For them the pre-existence of the soul before entering in a human life may be as crucial as is the afterlife to us. In the folk beliefs of Eastern European Jews the soul was believed to have existed since creation, waiting to be born, and just before birth an angel would take it on a journey through all time and space and then, at the moment before birth, would give it a blow which wiped all trace of this knowledge from memory. Among the Palestinian Arabs angels brought earth as well as a soul at conception, and the being so formed spent its early life traveling toward the place from which the earth came, for there its life would be ended. This interpretation gives a new and concrete poignancy to the words of the church burial service, "Dust thou art and unto dust thou shalt return." Perhaps even more widespread than the beliefs in immortality which conceive of a single sojourn in this world are those in which the human soul is conceived of as returning again and again. Some peoples see this return as a simple repetitive cycle which has always gone on since the beginning of the world and in which a man is reborn in one of his descendants—sometimes in the descendant who bears his name, sometimes only in someone in a designated generation. There are, of course, elaborations of these ideas in the great Eastern religions, in which the soul may enter lower forms than man and lives many lives, rewarded or punished for the way each life is lived by the nature of the next incarnation until, finally purified, it may escape the burden of further incarnations.

The second item in our picture of immortality—continued life in another sphere—has also many modifications. Many peoples think of the souls of their ancestors as staying near them, near their graves, or near the houses in which they have lived, or guarding the boundaries of ancestral lands, watching over the health and welfare of living kindred. In these beliefs death introduces another state of being, but the person lives on, disembodied, within the familiar earthly scene. Or when the next world is thought of as somehow in some other place—in the sky, within the earth, beneath the sea, or toward the sunset

—this may be conceived of as a condition of continuous, unchanging bliss, as when the Polynesian chiefs go to become pillars in the house of the gods, or as a state of frozen ecstasy, of eternal adoration of the Godhead, or as a world filled with events which will govern later incarnations, or as a world in which reward and punishment are differentiated. It seems to be a widespread characteristic of human beings that they are able to think more imaginatively about a hell than about a heaven, for while a desired next world may be pictured in terms of selected luxuries from this world or the details may not be specified at all, the tortures of the damned have been conceptualized over and over again with zest and vividness. It may well be that one measure of man's growing spiritual maturity, through the centuries in which his knowledge of the universe is deepend by exploration and experiment, will be a beginning ability to think as creatively about good as, in the past, he has thought about evil.

And third, there is the question of the persistence of identity. Our sense of personal identity is so strong that it seems inseparable from the idea of immortality. Yet many peoples see the problem quite differently. The Balinese have an Indonesian version of Hinduism and believe in a form of reincarnation within the same family line in an endless recurrence, from which escape is possible only for rajahs, for whom great ceremonies can be made, and for an occasional dedicated virgin worshiper. Souls, in an indeterminate number for each person, are reincarnated in great-grandchildren, and if a great-grandfather meets a great-grandchild on the street, he must pay him a penny, for he has no right to be alive at the same time. When someone dies in Bali, no one weeps. Only for an infant of a few months is a mother permitted to weep, and the relatives, as they dig the grave, are permitted to reproach it, "The next time you come, stay longer and at least eat rice with us before you go." The burial ceremonies include ritual practices to make the body more beautiful in the next incarnation, but all sense of personal identity disappears. One may compromise one's next incarnation either on this earth or in the dim purgatory where the dead await the next incarnation. A long run of bad luck may be blamed on debts that one of one's souls contracted during its stay in the other world, and people will say, "I am having bad luck this incarnation." Or, in giving to a beggar, they may re-mark, "I would not dare not to give to him. Who knows when I may not be as he? We all take turns." And a mother will say to a son who shows a sudden interest in gambling, "The reincar-nated soul in you must have been a great gambler!" But it is all quite impersonal, for there is no individual identity involved. This lack of a sense of identity is so marked that no one can describe the looks or manners of a person who died only a short time before. The body dies completely; the souls join other souls and return.

But the disposal of the body is a terrible problem for the Balinese. In ceremony after ceremony they seek to eliminate it finally. In the full cycle, there is first burial or a long period of keeping and guarding the corpse and then cremation. From the ashes, the bones are picked out and are reconstituted in the form of the skeleton, are dressed and laid out again in a minia-ture village in the graveyard; the souls, in the form of little figures carried by young girls as if they were babies, are taken home to the household temple, are given refreshment, and then are returned to the bones. Then the bones are pounded to ashes and are deposited in special containers which again represent human form. These in turn are burned and the result-ing ashes are taken down to the shore and sent out to sea in tiny canoes. Forty-two days later a new representation—this time with no material link to the old body—will be reconstituted to represent the souls, now become part of a household pantheon to whom their descendants pray. So, breaking the tie with the body is a condition of keeping the tie to the souls, but the sense of identity is only ceremonial.

In sharp contrast were the beliefs of the lagoon-dwelling people of the Admiralty Islands as recently as 1929. Here, souls, which came into being at conception, led their most vigorous and powerful lives immediately after death when a male became the overlord of the household of his immediate kin. His skull was kept in the rafters and, through diviners and mediums, he made his wishes known, rewarded and punished his kin for sins of omission and commission, and wreaked havoc among neighbors with whom they became involvd in economic disputes. But his reign, during which he married and sometimes had ghostly children, lasted only as long as he was able to protect the living males in his household from the malice of other ghosts. When the next male died, he was deposed, his skull was thrown out, and he became a homeless, malicious inhabitant of the lagoon, first a member of a set of anonymous kin ghosts, then a sea slug, and finally, after a few generations when all memory of his period on earth was gone also, he ceased to exist. When the Manus decided to become Christians, they pitched all the skulls of their guardian ghosts into the sea, deposing at once all of their regnant dead. Today they have a new culture which has incorporated many Western ideas, a local version of Christianity at present blessed by no mission, and an eager desire to multiply and become as numerous as the Americans who streamed, a million strong, through their islands during World War II; and they have invented the idea of reincarnation. Finding it wasteful to leave the souls of infants in heaven—as the mission taught them—they now pray to God to send them back in reincarnated form. Thus, in the space of a few years, they have moved from an extreme view of the mortality of highly identified individuals who were given a brief afterlife which was followed by annihilation, through an acceptance of orthodox Christian beliefs in an afterlife, to a new version of reincarnation.

A third relationship between immortality and identity is illustrated by the Iatmul of the Sepik River, a New Guinea mainland people, among whom reincarnation follows names and goes down in family lines. A prominent Yatmul man will be telling a story about some semimythical ancestral figure who bore the same name as the storyteller; in the middle of the tale he will shift from the third person to the first and say, "I was on the prow of that canoe," and as he speaks, he will stamp his foot on the floor of the house. The Iatmul sense of identity has a dream-like impersonal character in which role and individual existence are separated; a twelve-year-old boy, asked to tell the story of his life, will start to relate the events of childhood and then suddenly will be heard to say, "And then I married a woman of Wampun and had three children and the eldest was named . . ." Without noticing it, he has passed himself and gone on into a future which is as clear for him, because it is equally clearly socially defined, as is his past. So the Iatmul will relate elaborate events filled with the details of appropriate conversations and acts—which careful research shows never occurred at all—in the sense in which we, with our sense of actuality anchored in an irreversible, directional universe, would say that an event had occurred.

The persistence of identity not only is tied up in various ways with role, kin position, name, and the body—especially the less corruptible parts of the body, the bones—but it is related also in many different ways to the conception of the continued existence of the soul either as beneficial or harmful to the survivors or as the primary concern of the individual himself. Characteristically, in societies where ideas of religious development of the individual are crude and rudimentary, beliefs about the soul reflect a concern with the living and the terms of their grief. Human grief has many components: anger at being forsaken, guilt over hostile acts which have been left unatoned for and unforgiven, a passionate desire to capture and keep the memory of the departed, a desire to be rid of the reminder of one's own mortality. Different peoples have taken parts of this complex and have elaborated them. Among the Bagobo of the Philippines, in an area of the world where multiple souls are common, the people distinguish a good soul and a bad. At death the bad soul becomes a demon who feeds on the dead body, tearing it with its fingernails, and the good soul goes to a heaven where "the rice is of immaculate whiteness, and each grain is as big as a kernel of corn; the camotes are the size of a great wash pot, and every stick of sugar cane is as large as the trunk of a cocoanut palm." So people can make offerings to the good soul and attach to it all their positive feelings about the dead, while their negative feelings go into hatred and fear of the bad soul.

Some people emphasize only the hatred and fear, and go through elaborate ceremonies to separate themselves from the dead, deceiving the soul so that it will never be able to find its way back, cutting the throat of the corpse in a violent attempt to do away with the dead finally and forever. Within the tradition of Christian mourning only the positive feelings are emphasized; people weep for the dead as deeply and unambivalently loved, and those who harbor hatred and resentment feel guilty because of the inappropriate emotions which they must repress. Many primitive peoples have developed ritual exercises to ensure a proper display of agonized grief, such as cutting off a finger at the death of a relative. Grief so displayed may also be an essential propitiation, for the dead are expected to take revenge for unexpressed negative attitudes which the excessive mourning only masks.

Whether it is a question of banishing the dead or of keeping them close, the form of immortality is closely tied up with the role of the living. However, persistence of identity may also be envisaged as a personal goal, expressed either in a desire for continued identity—even in the same body—in the afterlife or in alternative technically secular forms in which the individual craves or is accorded immortality through the continued repercussions on earth of his acts while alive. These secular forms of immortality—through historic acts, generous bequests, or artistic or scientific creativity—appear to present a kind of negative counterbalance to literal and vivid expectations of immortality in another world. Visions of heaven become pallid and abstract as a man plans to live through his children—"the only immortality we have" or through buildings and discoveries, paintings or books, that bear his name. Conversely, a preoccupation with one's spiritual life and a belief that the main task of men on earth is "to colonize heaven," as an English bishop phrased it, tend to be accompanied by a negative attitude to the things of this world, including fame and creativity. But the line is seldom clear. A Burmese scholar once told me about the destruction of his life's scholarly work in a bombing during the war. "It is bad," he said, "for history, but good for me, as it detaches me from this world." And in England a study by Geoffrey Gorer shows that one out of seven people believe in some sort of reincarnation, because, they rationalize, one life doesn't give one a fair chance.

Thus, whether identity is to be cherished or escaped from, whether this life on earth is an intermediate state, a beginning or a recurrent episode in man's existence in the universe, whether, at death, the emphasis is upon the personal spiritual fate of the individual or upon the bereaved, whether the tie to this world is expressed in a belief in the resurrection of the body or in the persistence of a man's contribution to human culture, men's views of immortality become a framework within which earthly ways of life are judged and changed, lived and abandoned. A long life on earth is important to those who are concerned with taking a fully developed personality into the next world where all further development will cease and only eternal rewards and punishments remain. But the briefest sojourn as a day-old infant may be sufficient to attain a place in another world in which development is possible. The Soviet Communists, who have proclaimed their militant materialism, speak of a place in History, as a man fulfills the role assigned to him by History and so attains a sort of immortality—in History—with burial in the Red Wall. Modern medicine and public health practices flourish among those peoples for whom a long life in this world is a principal value; they are harder to introduce among peoples for whom the earth is a passing prelude to an impersonal eternity.

At an International Astronautical Congress in Rome some years ago Pope Pius XII blessed interplanetary exploration, within which man would work out new relationships to God and His universe. As we widen our sense of man's potentialities through our widening knowledge of the cosmos, the question of the immortality of man may be expected to widen also and to take on new forms.

Acknowledgments

The author wishes to thank the publishers of the periodicals and books listed below for permission to include in this volume in part or in altered form material drawn from earlier lectures and publications between 1951 and 1971.

Chapter I: "Cherishing the Life of the World." In *Pastoral Psychology*, No. 104 (May, 1960), 10-11.

Address delivered at the First Annual Meeting of the Academy of Religion and Mental Health, January 15, 1960.

Chapter II: "Introduction." In *Christians in a Technological Era*, ed. Hugh C. White, Jr. New York: Seabury Press, 1964, 11-23.

Chapter III: "Christian Faith and Technical Assistance." In *Christianity and Crisis*, 14, No. 23 (January 10, 1955), 179-182.

Chapter IV: "Cultural Man." In *Man in Community*, ed. Egbert De Vries. London: SCM Press; New York: Association Press, 1966, 197-217.

Chapter V: "20th Century Faith Must Use Technology." In *Methodist Woman*, 27, No. 4 (December, 1966), 9-11.

Chapter VI: "Neighbourhoods and Human Needs." In *Ekistics*, 21, No. 123 (February, 1966), 124-126. Center of Ekistics, Athens, Greece.

172 | TWENTIETH CENTURY FAITH

Chapter VII: "Spiritual Issues in the Problem of Birth Control." In *Pastoral Psychology*, 4, No. 34 (May, 1953), 39–44.

Chapter VIII: "The Liberal Church in an Urban Community." In *Journal of the Liberal Ministry*, 4, No. 2 (Spring, 1964), 65–73.
The William Ellery Channing Memorial Lecture, delivered at the Arlington Street Church, Boston, March 11, 1962.

Chapter IX: "A Religious System with Science at Its Very Core. . . ." In *Look*, 34, No. 8 (April, 1970), 37.

Chapter X: "The Future as the Basis for Establishing a Shared Culture." In *Daedalus* (Winter, 1965), 135–155.

Chapter XI: "Promise," "The Kalinga Prize" Lecture. In *Journal of World History*, Vol. XIII, No. 4 (1971), pp. 765–771, UNESCO.

Chapter XII: "Celebration: A Human Need." In *Catechist*, 1, No. 6 (March, 1968), 7–9.

Chapter XIII: "Cultural Contexts of Aging." In "What's Ahead for the Older American," *News: Union Settlement* (December, 1970).

Chapter XIV: "The Right To Die." In *Nursing Outlook*, 16, No. 10 (October, 1968), 20–21.

Chapter XV: "Ritual Expression of the Cosmic Sense." In *Worship*, 40, No. 2 (February, 1966), 66–72. O.S.B. Monks of St. John's Abbey, Collegeville, Minn.

Chapter XVI: "The Immortality of Man." In *Pastoral Psychology*, 8, No. 75 (June, 1957), 17–22.
Delivered in Lancaster, Pa., December 3, 1956, as the 17th Garvin Free Lecture.